The World and Its Wonders

The World and Its Wonders

DR. PAUL E. BLACKWOOD

DR. ROBERT M. GARRELS

MARGARET McKOWN STEPHENS

YVONNE BECKWITH, *Editor*

ANNE NEIGOFF, *Managing Editor*

STANDARD EDUCATIONAL CORPORATION   *Chicago 1985*

Library of Congress Cataloging in Publication Data
Blackwood, Paul Everett, 1913-
  The world and its wonders.

  (Child horizons)
  Includes index.
  1. Science—Juvenile literature. I. Garrels,
Robert Minard, 1916-   joint author.
II. Stephens, Margaret McKown, joint author.
III. Title.
Q163.B653   1978   500   78-3707
ISBN 0-87392-109-7

Rockets away! That is the call of the space age. There are man-made moons called satellites in the sky today and man has set them there. Today we dream of traveling to the far planets—and perhaps you will be one of the space explorers of the future who make that dream come true.

Once the thought of space exploration was only a fantastic dream. Yet for thousands of years, men have looked up at the sun and moon and stars and wondered about them. They asked questions and tried to find answers. You will find many of these answers in the pages of this book.

Men wondered about the great seas, too. Once they believed that dragons and other strange monsters lived in the depths of the oceans. Today we know there are no dragons. But there is still much for us to learn about the mysteries of the undersea world, and as we explore we are discovering exciting secrets.

Rivers and mountains, air currents and sound waves hold exciting secrets, too. The wind and rain and weather affect the way we live and how we live. There is much to find out and know and scientists of many kinds are working to give us this knowledge.

The world of science is wide and wonderful. When you watch television or put on a plastic raincoat, you are using products of scientific discovery. When you ride in an elevator or cross a bridge or drive in a car along a highway, you are using the result of a scientific experiment, too.

Perhaps one of the most wonderful things about science is that every scientific discovery started in exactly the same way. Someone asked a question. Why does this happen? How can I make that happen? Then the scientist tested and experimented until he found the answer.

You, too, can be part of the world of science. When you are puzzled, you can ask a question. And you can search until you find the answer. It is exciting to explore the world of space. It is even more exciting to explore the world of knowledge.

Table of Contents

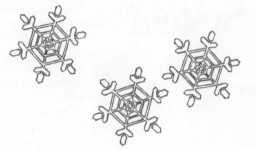

The Metric System

Two major systems of measurement are in use in the world today—the U.S. Customary System and the metric system. The U.S. Customary System uses such units as inches, feet, miles, pints, quarts, gallons, ounces, and pounds. The metric system uses three fundamental, or basic, units: meters (abbreviated m), for length; liters (l), for capacity; and grams (g), for weight.

Almost all countries of the world use a form of the metric system called the SI, or International System of Units. (SI is an abbreviation for the system's name in French, Système International d'Unités.) The SI has been used in the United States for scientific work for many years, and since the mid-1970's the country has been gradually converting to the SI for general use as well.

In addition to the fundamental units—the meter, liter, and gram—the metric system also has smaller and larger units. These units are identified by a uniform set of prefixes. The following list shows some of these prefixes, their abbreviations (in parentheses), and their relationship to the fundamental unit:

milli-   (m) — 1/1000 of the fundamental unit
centi-   (c) — 1/100 of the fundamental unit
deci-   (d) — 1/10 of the fundamental unit
deka-   (dk) — 10 times the fundamental unit
hecto-   (h) — 100 times the fundamental unit
kilo-   (k) — 1000 times the fundamental unit

Thus, 1 centimeter (cm) is 1/100 of a meter (or 10 millimeters or 1/10 of a decimeter); 1 milliliter (ml) is 1/1000 of a liter; and 1 kilogram (kg) is 1000 grams.

In the SI, the unit used to measure heat is the degree Celsius (°C) rather than the degree Fahreheit (°F.) used in the U.S. Customary System. Information on these two units is given on page 114.

The tables on the next page show how to convert common units from one system to the other. The conversion numbers, except for those for Fahrenheit and Celsius, are rounded for quick figuring, so the results are only approximate.

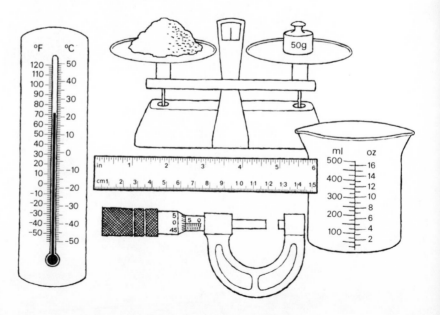

U.S. to Metric	Units	Examples
	1 inch = 25 millimeters	3 inches × 25 = 75 mm
	1 foot = 30 centimeters	3 feet × 30 = 90 cm
	1 foot = 0.3 meters	5 feet × 0.3 = 1.5 m
	1 yard = 0.9 meters	20 yards × 0.9 = 18 m
	1 mile = 1.6 kilometers	20 miles × 1.6 = 32 km
	1 square mile = 2.6 square kilometers	10 square miles × 2.6 = 26 sq km
	1 ounce (weight) = 28 grams	3 ounces × 28 = 84 g
	1 pound = 0.45 kilograms	15 pounds × 0.45 = 6.75 kg
	1 ounce (liquid) = 30 millileters	12 ounces × 30 = 360 ml
	1 pint = 0.47 liters	3 pints × 0.47 = 1.41 l
	1 quart = 0.95 liters	2 quarts × 0.95 = 1.9 l
	1 gallon = 3.8 liters	3 gallons × 3.8 = 11.4 l
Metric to U.S.	1 millimeter = .04 inches	35 mm × .04 = 1.4 inches
	1 centimeter = .4 inches	10 cm × .4 = 4 inches
	1 meter = 3.3 feet	20 m × 3.3 = 66 feet
	1 kilometer = .6 miles	30 km × .6 = 18 miles
	1 square kilometer = .4 square miles	75 sq km × .4 = 30 square miles
	1 gram = .04 ounces	30 g × .04 = 1.2 ounces
	1 kilogram = 2.2 pounds	60 kg × 2.2 = 132 pounds
	1 milliliter = 0.03 ounces	50 ml × 0.03 = 1.5 ounces
	1 liter = 1.05 quarts	5 l × 1.05 = 5.25 quarts

An exact conversion of degrees Fahrenheit to degrees Celsius is obtained as follows:

(Degrees Fahrenheit − 32) × 5/9 = Degrees Celsius

Example: 41° F. − 32 = 9

5/9 × 9 = 45/9 = 5° C.

An exact conversion of degrees Celsius to degrees Fahrenheit is obtained as follows:

(Degrees Celsius × 9/5) + 32 = Degrees Fahrenheit

Example: 20° C. × 9/5 = 180/5 = 36

36 + 32 = 68° F.

Whirling in Space

WE NEVER are still. Every minute of our lives we are on the go. Even while lifting a glass of water from the table to our lips we travel 30 or 40 miles. The earth and everything on it moves 18½ miles each second of the day and of the night as the earth travels through space in its orbit or circle-like journey around the sun.

We always are moving from west to east, too, because the earth turns completely around on its own axis every 24 hours. This double movement is much like that of a top that is spinning and at the same time making a wide sweep around the room.

You may wonder at the thought of this earth of ours moving in these different ways and at such speeds. But this has been going on for many millions of years before you were born and will no doubt continue for as many more millions of years in the future. We cannot see or feel these motions of the earth, although we do see and feel the effects of them. We know, too, that the earth like everything else in the universe follows an orderly pattern. We can go to bed in the darkest night, feeling sure that there will be daylight at a certain time in the morning. We know that spring follows winter and summer follows spring. The reasons why these things occur as they do are more interesting than a fairy tale.

Earth & Sky

You may wonder, too, why we do not fall off the earth while we are traveling at such speeds. We surely would if something did not hold us on. This something is called the force or pull of gravity. We cannot see gravity but we know that it exists. Every time we throw a ball into the air it comes back down to us. We cannot stay up in the air without a support under us because gravity pulls us down, just as though a magnet were in the center of the earth drawing us toward it. It is the pull of gravity that gives us weight.

A long time ago people believed the earth was flat. They thought that if a ship sailed out to sea far enough, it would go over the edge of the world, fall off into space, and be lost forever. They thought the earth was the center of the universe and that the sun, moon, and stars moved around it. They felt certain of this because they could see that the heavenly bodies moved across the sky.

As time went on there were men who were not satisfied with these explanations. Some began to think that the earth was round like a ball. But until Christopher Columbus came along no one had the courage to sail across the ocean to try to prove it. And while he did not exactly prove that the earth is round, he convinced others who soon did prove it.

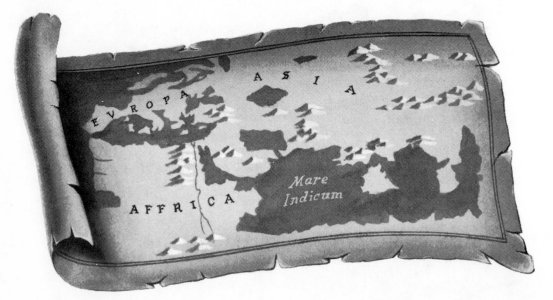

Map of known world at the time of Columbus.

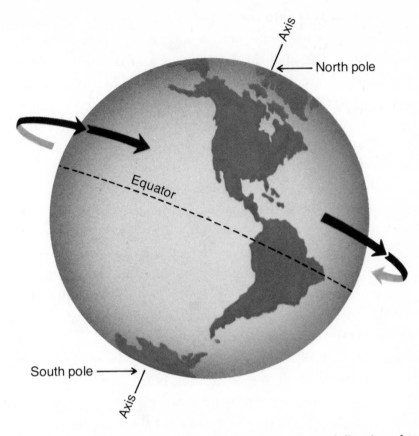

Western hemisphere showing the earth's equator, poles, axis, and direction of turning

Later, people learned that the earth itself turns around every 24 hours and that it is one of several planets that revolve around the sun. Then it was possible to explain a great many things that never could be understood before, such as what happened to the sun at night. It was the turning of the earth that made the sun and the other heavenly bodies *seem* to move across the sky.

The earth looks flat because we can see only a small part of it at one time. Still if we were to travel far enough in the same direction we would come back to the place where we started. In the days of sailing vessels this was hard to prove, but, today, airplanes regularly circle the globe. Perhaps the best proof of the earth's roundness has been the photographs of our planet taken from space by astronauts traveling between the earth and the moon.

Suppose we let an orange represent the earth. Then, let us insert a small stick part way into the top of the orange and another into the bottom exactly opposite the first one. The spot where the top stick enters the orange is called the North Pole, and the bottom stick marks the South Pole. Imagine a line running straight through the center of the orange between these two places. This line is called the *axis*. Imagine another line running around the outside of the orange at its center, halfway between the two poles. This is called the *Equator*.

The diameter of the earth (that is, the distance straight through its center) at the Equator is 7,926 miles. The length of its axis is 27 miles less, showing that the earth is just slightly flattened at the poles. The earth's circumference (the distance around it) at the Equator is 24,902 miles. On some maps the earth is divided into halves, or hemispheres. Thus we speak of the Northern Hemisphere and the Southern Hemisphere or the Eastern and Western Hemispheres, depending on which way we divide it. North and South America belong in what is considered the Western Hemisphere.

Taking one of the sticks in the fingers of each hand, turn the orange slowly. Your model earth is now turning on its axis. You can see that points near the Equator are moving more rapidly than points nearer the poles. In fact, a point on the earth near the Equator moves at the rate of about 17 miles a minute, while a point near Chicago, 3,000 miles north of the Equator, or Wellington, New Zealand, 3,000 miles south of the Equator, moves at the rate of only about 12 miles a minute.

Now, suppose you mark a tiny spot on the orange to show about where you live. Never mind if you do not get it just right because almost any spot will do. With a small light, such as a candle or a flashlight, in a darkened room you can see the appearance of day and night quite clearly as you turn the orange, or earth, on its axis. When your spot on the earth is toward the candle which, of course, we are pretending is the sun, you are in the light and it is day, and when it is on the opposite side, you are in the dark and it is night. Do you understand why the sun comes up on the side toward which the earth is turning and goes across the sky to the west, and at night the stars move across in the same direction? You can see now that it is the earth's turning which makes it look as though the sun and stars were moving.

As the earth spins around from west to east the side that is toward the sun is constantly changing. The sun "rises," that is, daylight comes when the earth has rotated on its axis far enough to bring us within the light of the sun. As we turn farther eastward the sun seems to climb in the sky until it seems nearly overhead. At that point we say it is noon. Noon comes at the exact moment when the sun appears to pass from the eastern to the western half of the sky. As the earth continues to revolve the spot on which we live begins to turn away from the sun. This causes the sun to appear to sink lower and lower in the western sky until it finally "sets." Then night begins. It will continue until the earth turns around far enough for the sun's rays to strike us again.

Before clocks were invented, men experimented until they found ways of telling time. They noticed the different positions and lengths of shadows at different times of the day. They invented the sundial consisting of a stick or post which cast a shadow on a dial with the

Night and Day

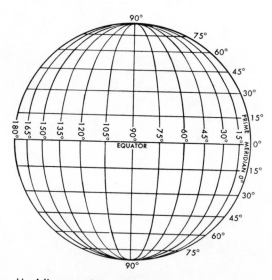

Hourglass and sundial—old ways of telling time.

hours marked around it. But when the sun was not shining, the sundial would not work. Other devices were used, and later the hourglass was made. This consisted of two closed containers joined by a narrow neck through which sand or some other substance slowly poured. Just enough of this material was put in so that it would take an hour for it to run from one container to the other. When it had all run out, the hourglass was turned over so that it would run back again during the next hour.

The correct time that we hear over the radio every day is based on signals sent out by the United States Naval Observatory, where it is obtained by checking the position of the earth in relation to the stars. Our watches may stop, or lose or gain a little, but the turning of the earth is always exactly on time. It is from the speed of its turning that our time is reckoned.

As a circle is divided into 360 equal parts, or degrees, the distance around the

Meridians and parallels at 15° intervals.

16

earth's surface is for many purposes expressed in degrees. Degrees of a circle, like degrees of temperature, are usually written by a symbol that looks like a small zero after the number. Thus 90 degrees is written 90°. The accepted starting point for measuring distances east and west, called longitude, and also for reckoning time is the *prime* meridian, a half circle between the poles running through Greenwich, England. In the same way distances north or south, with the Equator as the dividing line, are measured in degrees of latitude. While a degree of longitude is about 70 miles at the Equator you

TIME ZONES
of the United States

can see that it becomes less and less as one goes north or south.

Since it takes the earth 24 hours to make one complete rotation, each 15° westward is an hour later in time, 1° meaning a difference of 4 minutes. To avoid confusion and the inconvenience of adjusting timepieces more frequently, the world is divided into hourly time belts or zones about 15° wide. Thus, when we travel eastward or westward, we merely set our watches ahead or behind one hour at a time as we cross the line from one zone to another. There are four such zones in the United States—Eastern, Central, Mountain, and Pacific. When it is 12 o'clock noon in New York, many people in Los Angeles are having a late breakfast, for there it is only 9 o'clock.

17

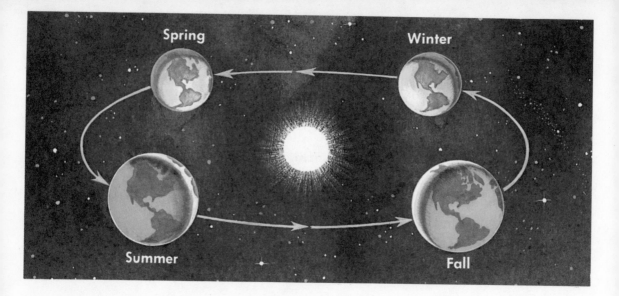

Journey Around the Sun

LONG ago people thought the sun was a god. They worshiped it because they knew it gave them light to see by and heat to warm their bodies and to ripen their crops. Today we know that the sun is a whirling, glowing ball of hot gases and that it is really a star, our day star. It is at the center of the vast orbits, or paths, in which the earth and the other planets travel through space.

In fact, the earth actually is controlled by the sun. Just as the earth's gravity holds everything on the earth to it, the force of gravity of the sun holds the earth in its path around the sun. It is the sun and not the earth that is the center of our part of the universe. And it is well for us that this is so. Without the sun, the earth would be a terribly cold, dark place. Nothing could grow on it. No one could live on it.

In comparison with the size of the sun, the earth is very small. In terms of diameters, it would take 109 of our earths in a row to extend across the diameter of the sun. But in terms of volume or total space occupied, it would take more than 1,000,000 globes the size of the earth to make a globe the size of the sun. It is the great distance from us that makes the sun look as small as it does. It is 93,000,000 miles away.

In the previous story we learned that the spinning of the earth on its axis brings us night and day. This story will tell more about the other important motion of the earth, its long journey around the sun. It is this movement that brings us our seasons—spring, summer, autumn or fall as it is commonly called, and winter. It takes the earth 365¼ days to make the complete trip and this gives us our year.

The earth's axis is not straight up and down in relation to its path around the sun but tilted 23½° from that position, so first one pole and then the other faces the sun. If it were not tilted, there would be no change of seasons, as each part of the earth would receive the same amount of light and heat every month of the year. As it is, during that part of the year in which the Northern

Dot shows size of earth as compared to size of sun represented by white circle.

Hemisphere is tilted toward the sun, we have summer, while at the same time it is winter below the Equator because the Southern Hemisphere is then tilted away from the sun. On the other hand, as the earth gets around to the other side of its orbit, the Southern Hemisphere is tilted toward the sun and the people there are having summer, while we in the northern half of the world get less sunlight and are having winter.

Suppose you use the orange for the earth with the sticks placed at the poles again and let a grapefruit represent the sun. Have someone hold the grapefruit in his outstretched hand. With the orange tilted as in the picture on the opposite page, turn it on its axis, and at the same time move it slowly in a wide circular sweep around the grapefruit.

Remember always to keep the sticks in the orange pointing in the same direction, just as the earth's axis is always in line with the North Star, regardless of the motion of the earth. You are showing the journey the earth makes every year. When you have gone around once and reached the point you started from, a year has passed. Notice that part of the time the North Pole is more directly toward the sun but when the earth gets around to the other side of its orbit, the South Pole is tipped toward the sun.

Winter brings snow and cold.

There are two points in this yearly journey where the two hemispheres get an equal amount of sunshine, with neither pole pointing toward the sun more than the other. At these points, it is the Equator that exactly faces the sun. These two times each year are at the end of winter and the beginning of spring, about March 21; and the end of summer and the beginning of fall, about September 23. On these occasions day and night are equal, each being 12 hours long, all over the world. Then for all points on the Equator, at noon the sun is directly overhead.

When the Northern Hemisphere is turned toward the sun, more of this half of the world is in daylight. Our days then are longer and the nights shorter. The opposite is true at this same time in the Southern Hemisphere, just as our nights are longer and our days are shorter in winter. And we not only have less hours of daylight in winter but, when the earth is tilted away from the sun, the rays strike us at more of a slant, so they give us less heat.

You know how much lower the sun appears in the sky in winter than in summer and how much less warmth the sun has then. Likewise the sun's rays are not nearly as hot in the early morning or late afternoon as they are when the sun is nearly overhead. These slanting rays do not warm us so much because as they strike the earth they spread out over a wider area and have less effect on any one spot.

Summer brings grass and flowers.

You can see how this is when on a dark night you point a flashlight straight at your feet. You then get a bright light on a small spot; but if you tilt the light in order to cover 30 or 40 feet of the pathway ahead of you, no spot gets much light because the same amount of light is spread over more space.

The sun is not only exactly overhead at the Equator twice each year but, near the Equator, the noonday sun is never far from overhead. There the days and nights are never far from equal in length regardless of what the seasons may be farther north or south. Thus the temperature is much the same there the year around. It is always hot summer weather.

As we go north or south away from the Equator, the weather varies. There is winter and summer. When it is winter in the Northern Hemisphere, a large area around the North Pole cannot possibly get any sunlight, regardless of the spinning of the earth, because it is turned away from the sun. There are several months when that part of the earth does not have any daylight at all. At the same time a similar area around the South Pole is having constant daylight with no night. When the earth gets around to the opposite side of its orbit, those conditions are reversed. Thus the winters in the Far North or the Far South are not only very cold, but they also are in continual darkness. Those same places in summer are in constant daylight but, as the sun's rays even then are quite slanting, the polar regions never receive a great deal of heat.

Thus we see that the earth's journey around the sun brings the changes of season to the different parts of the earth, and that some parts of it are affected much more than others.

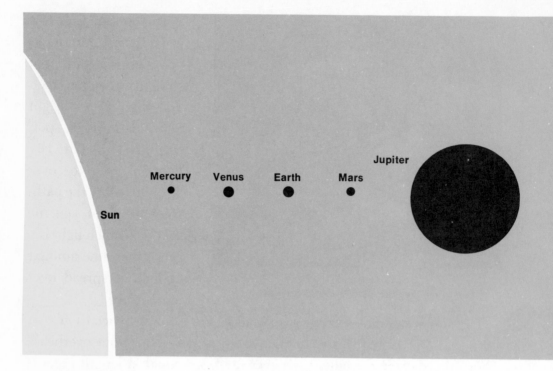

The Other Planets

THE EARTH is one of nine planets. Like the other eight, it is controlled by the sun and revolves about it. All the planets move in the same direction, but each at a different distance from the sun. And, although they are said to belong to the same family and act alike in many ways, they are quite different in others, just as brothers or sisters often are.

Some planets, since they are closer to the sun than others, are very hot while those far away are very cold. Some are smaller than the earth and some are much larger. As the length of a day on any planet is the time that it takes to rotate once on its axis and the lengh of a year is the time that it takes to revolve once in its orbit around the sun, all have days and years of different lengths.

The force of gravity is also quite different on the various planets. A 100-pound boy would weigh only 37 pounds on Mercury and 38 pounds on Mars, while on Jupiter he would weigh 264 pounds. Some planets have no air around them and very little moisture. How many problems we would have if the dream of some people should come

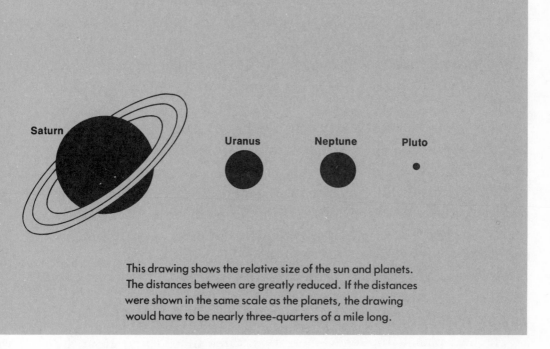

Saturn Uranus Neptune Pluto

This drawing shows the relative size of the sun and planets.
The distances between are greatly reduced. If the distances
were shown in the same scale as the planets, the drawing
would have to be nearly three-quarters of a mile long.

true—that one day we might step into a spacecraft and visit another planet!

The smallest planet is Mercury, just a little larger than our moon. It is also the planet nearest to the sun. Being the nearest, Mercury has the shortest journey around the sun; also its speed is the greatest. And, of course, it is the hottest, at least it has the hottest day. As compared with our year of 365 days, it takes Mercury only 88 days to make one complete trip around the sun. But Mercury turns only once on its axis every 59 days, meaning that its day is two-thirds as long as its year. Photographs of Mercury taken from unmanned spacecraft show that the planet is covered with many craters, much like the earth's moon. When Mercury can be seen from the earth, which is not often because it is so near the sun, it appears in the western sky right after sunset or in the eastern sky just before sunrise. It then looks as bright as a star.

Venus is next and is about twice as far from the sun as Mercury. It is almost as large as the earth, and its orbit is closer to the earth's than any other planet. For this reason, Venus was the first planet to which the unmanned spacecraft were sent. Several of these craft actually landed on the surface of Venus, where they recorded temperatures as high as 900° Fahrenheit. Scientists believe that life as we know it could not exist on Venus.

Venus turns even more slowly on its axis than does Mercury. One full day is about 243 earth days, or about 18 earth days longer than Venus's year!

After Venus comes the earth, then Mars, which is often called the Red Planet because of its appearance in the night sky. The orbit of Mars is beyond that of the earth, and Mars takes almost twice as long to go around the sun as the earth takes. If there is life on any planet in the solar system other than the earth, it is probably on Mars. The Red Planet is not as warm as the earth, and the nights and winters are extremely cold. Moreover, there is very little oxygen in the atmosphere. The day on Mars is about the same length as ours. Mars has two tiny moons, about 10 to 15 miles in diameter, which travel around the planet much as our moon circles the earth.

The next planet, Jupiter, is more than three times as far from the sun as Mars is. Jupiter is truly the giant of the planets, containing more matter than the other eight planets put together. Jupiter spins very rapidly on its axis, making a complete rotation in less than 11 hours. Seen through a telescope, Jupiter shows a surface marked with many colored bands, which are actually the tops of dense clouds. The giant planet has 13 known moons, of which 4 are about as large as our moon.

Saturn is nearly as large as Jupiter and almost twice as far from the sun. Through a telescope, Saturn can be seen to have a series of bright rings around it. These rings are probably made up of rocks of various sizes. Saturn has 10 moons, of which one—Titan—is about the size of the planet Mercury and has an atmosphere.

Next comes Uranus, the farthest planet that can be seen without a telescope. It has five moons and is nearly twice as far from the sun as Saturn. Still farther away is Neptune. The temperature there must be very low, for Neptune is 30 times as far away from the sun as the earth.

Pluto is so far away that no one even suspected that it existed until the early 1900's and it was not sighted until 1930. Not much is known about it yet except that it takes about 250 years to make one trip around the sun, and that its diameter is probably less than half that of the earth.

The word planet means "wanderer" and it might seem at first, as it did to the ancient Greeks who gave them the name, that they wander about in space. In particular, the planets whose orbits are beyond that of the earth seem to wander across the night sky. For a time they seem to move eastward from night to night. Then they seem to stop and begin moving to the west. After a time, the entire sequence is repeated.

We can see only that part of any planet that is in a position to reflect sunlight toward us, since the planets, like the moon, have no light of their own. Also, they appear brighter as they get closer to the earth and dimmer as they get farther away in their wide sweeps around the sun. No wonder the ancient Greeks thought they were wanderers.

You can usually tell a planet from a star because the planets do not seem to twinkle as the stars do.

FACTS ABOUT THE PLANETS				
Planet	Diameter (in miles)	Distance from Sun (in millions of miles)	Length of Day (time required to rotate once on its axis)	Length of Year (time, in earth days and years, required to revolve around sun)
Mercury	3,032	36	59 earth days	88 days
Venus	7,521	67	243 earth days	224 days, 17 hours
Earth	7,926	93	1 day (24 hours)	365 days, 6 hours
Mars	4,217	142	24 hours, 37 minutes	687 days
Jupiter	88,700	484	9 hours, 50 minutes	11 years, 314 days
Saturn	74,600	887	10 hours, 14 minutes	29 years, 168 days
Uranus	32,200	1,783	10 hours, 49 minutes	84 years, 4 days
Neptune	30,800	2,794	16 hours	164 years, 292 days
Pluto	3,700	3,666	6 days, 9 hours	247 years, 256 days

An astronaut on the moon salutes the American flag. His space vehicle is in the center.

Space Explorers of the Moon

FOR thousands and thousands of years, mankind had a great dream. One day a man would go to the moon and walk on its far-away surface. On July 20, 1969, this age-old dream came true. Neil Armstrong, an American astronaut, became the first human to set foot on the moon. He spoke for all men, everywhere, when he said:

"That's one small step for a man, one giant leap for mankind."

All men, everywhere, can be proud of Neil Armstrong and astronauts Colonel Edwin Aldrin and Lieutenant Colonel Michael Collins who made that historic space voyage with him in *Apollo 11*.

That first step on the moon opened the way for other space voyages to the moon and other planets. It proved that mankind is no longer held fast to one planet, the earth.

Today men have circled the moon and sent back television pictures to show us the moon's surface. Men have walked on the moon and we have watched them on television as they did so. They have brought back samples of moon rocks to add to our knowledge of earth's only natural satellite, the moon.

Man-made satellites and rockets have also given us much information about the moon. But man's first knowledge about the moon came through the telescope.

Through a telescope, we can see that the moon's surface is rough and uneven. In many places, there are huge holes, or craters.

The moon has broad plains, too, which appear to us as darker patches. It is these plains that we imagine make up the face of the "man in the moon." If people lived on the moon and looked on our earth they undoubtedly would see pictures on it too. We often can see the moon in the daytime, although very faintly because the sky is then so bright. But whether we see it or not, it always has some effect on the earth. Its force of gravity exerts enough pull on the water of the ocean so that the moon is the chief cause of our tides.

The moon is much nearer to the earth than any other heavenly body and, except for the sun, it is the brightest. It is ruled by the earth and compelled by the earth's pull of gravity to go around it just as the earth is controlled by the sun and compelled to go in a wide circle-like sweep around the sun.

The moon is only about 240,000 miles away from us and while this is nearly as far as 10 times around our Equator, it is very little compared to the enormous distances between the planets and the sun and the stars. The sun is about 400 times as far from us.

The diameter of the moon is only 2,160 miles, about ¼ that of the earth, but because they are both in the shape of a ball, it would take about 50 moons to fill a globe the size of the earth. The reason why the moon looks about as large as the sun is that the moon is so very much closer to us.

The force of gravity of the moon is only ⅙ that of the earth, so a man weighing 180 pounds on the earth would weigh only 30 pounds there. However, we may be sure that no one lives on the moon as the conditions are such that no kind of life, either plant or animal as we know it, could possibly exist. There is practically no air or moisture, therefore there can be no clouds or winds, nothing to tone down the blinding sunshine of days that are two weeks long.

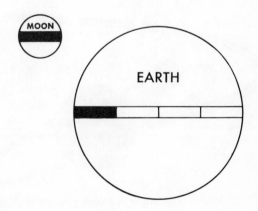

And the equally long nights must be very dark and intensely cold.

As our earth is turning on its axis and at the same time making its long yearly journey around the sun, the moon is turning on its own axis and also traveling in a path around the earth. The earth, you know, turns 365¼ times while it is making the trip around the sun. The moon makes just *one* turn on its axis during the 27⅓ days that it takes to go around the earth. Therefore, it always keeps the same side toward the earth.

Suppose you put a chair in the center of the room to represent the earth. Then pretend you are the moon and, walking sideways, step around the chair always facing toward it until you have gone once around. By so doing, you have slowly turned once at the same time that you were going around the chair, although your face was always toward the chair. A person sitting in the chair could not see your back. Except for the fact that the earth also is always moving, this is the way the moon goes around the earth.

Although we can see only one side of the moon from earth, rockets carrying special cameras have traveled around it and photographed the side of the moon we cannot see.

The moon has no light of its own. It shines by reflected sunlight. That is, as the sun's rays fall on the moon, some of the light is reflected to us. If the sun did not shine on the moon, we could not see it at all.

Once in a while, for a few minutes, the moon comes exactly between

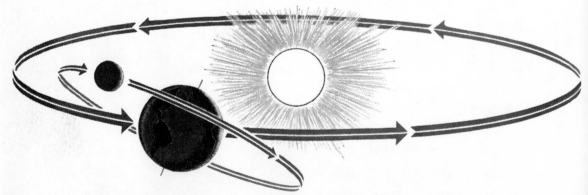

The moon revolves around the earth while the earth revolves around the sun.

us and the sun so that it blots out our view of the sun even during the day. When this happens the earth gets as dark as it does on a cloudy day. This is called an eclipse of the sun.

Sometimes, too, the moon happens to get on the opposite side of our planet so that the earth blocks the sun's rays to the moon. That is, the moon gets in the earth's shadow. We call this an eclipse of the moon and it may last for several hours.

You know that the sun shines on only half of the earth at one time. It also shines on only half of the moon, but from where we are, we cannot always see all of the section that is lighted. When the moon is almost in line with the sun, we cannot see it at all. The moon is then said to be new.

About two days later as the moon moves over slightly to one side there is a tiny strip along the edge toward the sun that shows to us. The moon then, still quite new, appears faintly as a thin crescent in the western sky just after the sun has gone down.

Each night the moon appears almost an hour later. As it moves over farther from the sun, more of the side that is in the sunlight can be seen so that its crescent

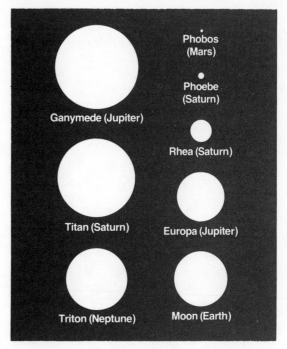

The earth's moon compared with some other moons of the solar system. Ganymede, the largest, is actually larger than the planet Mercury. Earth's moon is the sixth-largest moon in the solar system.

This photograph shows an eclipse of the sun. The photographer took pictures of the sun every seven minutes so we could see the eclipse in different stages.

Roy Swan, The Minneapolis Star

14.9 DAYS

7 DAYS

4.6 DAYS

shape becomes wider and wider. About a week after new moon, the moon looks like a capital D and this appearance or phase is called the first quarter. It has now gone ¼ of the way around the earth.

This shape becomes still wider as the moon gets farther from the sun until in about another week, the moon is in the position opposite the sun where we can see the entire lighted side.

22 DAYS

26.4 DAYS

Lick Observatory

Then the side that is always toward the earth is also directly toward the sun. It looks big and round and bright and we call it a full moon. The moon has now gone ½ of the way around the earth.

In a few nights the light will not be so bright for the moon will begin to wane or grow thinner. In another week's time when it has gone ¾ of the way around the earth, we will see only ½ of its face again. This is called the last quarter moon and looks like the first quarter moon turned around. From then on the crescent becomes thinner and thinner until it fades completely from sight.

While it has taken the moon only 27⅓ days to go around the earth, the earth also has been moving in its orbit around the sun. It takes a little longer, 29½ days in all, for the moon to go far enough to arrive at the position nearly in line with the sun where it is ready to start on its phases again. Do you see why a month is often referred to as a "moon"?

31

Twinkling Far Away

THE stars are other huge glowing balls like our sun. Many of them are much larger than the sun, and like it they give off light and heat. We can see their light, but we cannot feel their warmth because they are so very far away from the earth.

To get a better understanding of their enormous sizes and their distances from us, let us start with some of the things we have already learned. In the first story we used an orange to represent the earth. If we want to show the sun in its true size compared with the earth, we will have to let a two-car garage or something about that size represent the sun. And we will have to place the orange nearly one-half mile from the garage, so great is the distance of the earth from the sun. Our model, though, is already getting large and we have hardly started to measure the distance to the stars. Let us use some smaller objects for comparison.

Suppose we let a little pea represent the earth. Then we must use something very small, perhaps the head of a pin for the moon, and place it about ten inches from the pea. But we will need a giant pumpkin nearly three feet across to represent the sun, and it must be placed about a block away. Now we can see how enormously larger and farther away the sun is, as compared to the moon.

We could select other objects of appropriate sizes to represent the planets, prehaps an orange for Jupiter placed out about five blocks, and we might let another pea, if we can find a very small one, represent Pluto, but it would have to be placed two and one-half miles away.

Now let us consider the stars. Even on this scale, with the little pea representing the earth, the pinhead the moon, and the big pumpkin a block away the sun, we must imagine another pumpkin over 16,000 miles away in order to show the proper proportion of distance to the nearest star. Remember, this is to the *nearest* star. Most stars are much farther away, so far that we can hardly imagine the distance. On a clear, dark night we can see about 2,000 stars but there are millions of them that can be seen only through a powerful telescope. No doubt there are many millions beyond those that no one has ever been able to see.

In the last part of the sixteenth century, the great Italian scientist, Galileo, constructed a crude telescope and made many startling discoveries. With this instrument he saw that the moon was not a smooth object like a plate, as men before him had thought, but was ball-like and very rough. He saw spots on the sun that we know now, are caused by the explosion of gases. He learned that Venus goes through phases similar to the phases of our moon. He discovered that the four moons of Jupiter, which he could see, traveled around that planet. This had never before been known. From his early observations astronomers have gone ahead to study the stars.

The huge domed observatory
on the right is located at
Mt. Wilson, California.

Mt. Wilson Observatory

There are several telescopes at Mt. Wilson. This one is a
reflecting telescope. It contains a 60 inch mirror.

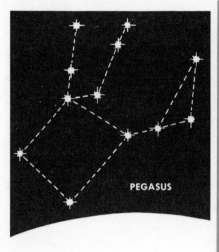

PEGASUS

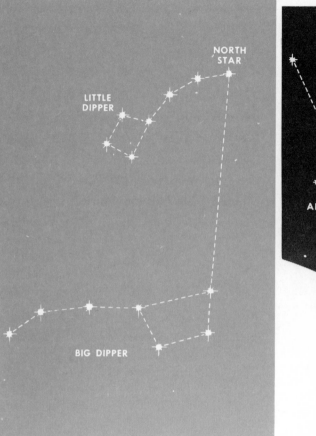

NORTH STAR

LITTLE DIPPER

BIG DIPPER

ARIES

The stars rise and set just as the sun and moon do because of the turning of the earth. In their rising and setting the stars always appear to have the same position in relation to one another. Because of this, it is fairly easy to distinguish between the stars and the planets. Scientists tell us that the stars do move in relation to each other, but they are so far away that the changes in their positions could not be detected by our unaided eyes even if we could watch the sky for several centuries. But with measurements made by the most accurate instruments, we find that the stars do change their positions gradually.

In the Northern Hemisphere, however, there is one star that we always see in the same position regardless of the turning of the earth because it happens to be directly in line with the North Pole and the axis of the earth. That is Polaris, commonly called the North Star.

It is easy to find because it is the brightest star in that part of the sky. But you can always locate the North Star from the Big Dipper which can be found somewhere in the north on any clear night. Two stars of the Big Dipper outline the portion of the bowl opposite the

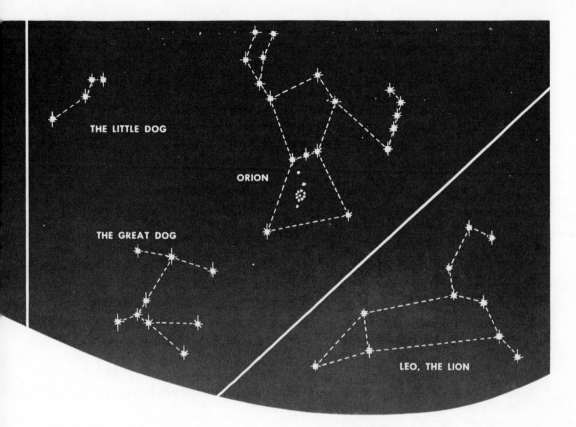

THE LITTLE DOG

ORION

THE GREAT DOG

LEO, THE LION

handle. They always point toward the North Star although the entire Big Dipper turns in a great circle in the northern sky once every 24 hours. There is also a Little Dipper. The North Star is the end star of its handle.

There are many other stars that appear together in groups. Since man first gazed upward, he found that certain groups made pictures. We call these groups constellations. The shepherds of long ago made up stories about the constellations as they watched their flocks at night. Orion and his Dogs, Leo the Lion, and Pegasus the Winged Horse are a few of the more common ones.

Many stories have been told, too, about the Milky Way. Some people thought that it was the road that led to Heaven. On a clear and moonless night the Milky Way shows very plainly. This long, ragged belt of faint white across the sky really is made up of millions of stars so far away that they look like a milky path.

35

This picture, taken through a telescope, shows the Horsehead Nebula. A nebula is a great cloud of dust and gas within our galaxy. Can you see why people named this the Horsehead Nebula?

Adler Planetarium

The Milky Way is a huge group of stars called a *galaxy*. We call the Milky Way our galaxy, because it is the home of our solar system. Our star, the sun, and its system of planets is a tiny, tiny part of this huge galaxy. The Milky Way Galaxy is so big that there is room in it for us, and billions of stars, and all the space between the stars.

Space distances are so enormous that it is hard to imagine the distance between one star and another.

The nearest star to earth, other than the sun, is 25 million million miles away. If you could travel one million miles an hour it would take you almost 3,000 years to reach this star!

And there are billions of stars in our galaxy, and each one has millions of miles of space between it and the next star. Can you see why it is hard to image how big our galaxy is?

But here is something that is even harder to imagine. Our galaxy is not the only one! There are millions and millions of galaxies, and each one has billions of stars!

No one knows how many stars and galaxies there are, but we say they all fit into a place called the *universe*. The universe is so unbelievably big that no one on our little earth can imagine its size.

Yerkes Observatory

The white streak in this picture is a meteor or shooting star.

"Falling Stars"

WHAT some people call "falling stars" or "shooting stars" are not stars at all. They are meteors—chunks of metal and rock that whirl about in space between the heavenly bodies somewhat like a handful of confetti thrown in front of an electric fan. Often one of these objects comes toward our planet. It may be a mere speck of dust, or the size of a pebble, or weigh several tons. As it nears the earth, the meteor rushes through the air which causes it to glow and appear to be a falling star.

A meteor falls rapidly, at the rate of from six to forty-five miles a second, and is usually burned out in a second or two. Once in a while a meteor is so large it does not burn itself out by the time it reaches the earth. Then it may hit the ground with such force that it makes a hole. That part of a meteor which falls to the ground is called a meteorite. In the desert in Arizona, there is a hole nearly a mile wide that was made by a huge meteorite.

Earth's Surface

The Birth and Life of a River

WHEN rain falls on the ground, it may soak in or it may run off. If it runs off, it will run toward lower ground, forming a little stream and meeting other little streams on the way. If much rain falls, the stream grows larger and deeper as it reaches still lower ground and other streams join with it. When the rain stops, the little streams dry up. But the ditch they have made remains and carries the water away at the next rainfall. With each rainfall the water washes more and more dirt away and the ditches become bigger and deeper. In time these streams even may cut their way through hard rock.

Smaller streams unite to form creeks; creeks run into small rivers, and small rivers run into larger rivers. This means that more and more water is carried by a single stream which usually flows toward the ocean. The Mississippi River is a good example of the way many streams unite to form a very large river.

Most of the water that helps form rivers comes from rain. But snow in northern climates, and snow that collects on mountain tops is another big source of river water. When the weather becomes warm the snow melts, and the water trickles down to lower levels and flows into streams.

United States Department of Interior   United States Department of Interior

Young river valley   Mature river valley

Another source of streams is *ground water*. Ground water is water that soaks into the ground when it rains or snows. It forms two underground zones. The upper zone usually has only a small amount of water in the spaces in the soil. The lower zone has all the spaces filled with water. The top of the lower zone is called the *water table*. When heavy rains fall, the water table rises nearer to the surface. When there is a long dry period, the water table sinks deep into the ground.

Heavy rains not only cause the water table to rise; they also cause the soil to wear away in river beds on top of the land. Sometimes this makes the streams on the surface meet the ground water below the surface. In this way streams get larger and become permanent rivers. There is usually a constant flow of water in streams that have cut into the ground below the water table except during the worst droughts.

There is another way that ground water joins rivers. On hillsides it sometimes seeps out and forms springs. This spring water may run directly down and help make a river or it may collect in a low basin and form a lake. When lakes overflow the water may run out and form a river. Although it is easier to see how rain and snow form rivers, ground water is an important river builder, too.

Century Photos, Inc.

Old river valley

There are a few rivers that developed in a different way. Ages and ages ago, the ocean helped form some of our rivers. Sometimes the land at the edge of the ocean sank; sometimes the floor of the ocean rose. The lowlands created became valleys and water flooded into them, making rivers. These are called *drowned valleys*. There are many along the eastern seacoast, especially in New England. The Hudson River is an example.

Rivers are *youthful, mature,* or *old*. When a river system is youthful, its streams cut almost straight downward. They form steep V-shaped valleys. Young streams are swift-flowing and usually have very crooked courses that bend, here and there, to fit themselves to the low places in the land. There are deep canyons, rugged cliffs, and steep ridges in a region that has many youthful streams.

Running water causes more wearing away of soil and rock or *erosion* than any other single force. After millions of years of stream erosion, a youthful river valley may become a mature river valley. Tributaries branch and rebranch. They cut through the ridges and high crests of land. The land becomes less rugged. The river valley curves less sharply and the water does not flow as fast. This kind of stream valley is called mature.

If stream erosion continues for more millions of years, the countryside will change again. The water will wear away the land until the river winds slowly across a nearly level plain. The water of the river will cut into the banks and widen the stream bed. Finally the river valley becomes broad and quiet. A river like this is called an old river.

A river may be youthful, mature, or old, but there is one very important way that all rivers are alike. They are always changing the face of the land.

Rivers have always been very important in helping people decide where to live. Most early settlements in the United States, for instance, grew up along river banks because the river provided people with necessities like water and transportation. In some places the nature of a river determined the location of the first villages. Some of the early settlers sailed their ships up rivers along the Atlantic coast until they were stopped by rapids and falls. They could go no further so they settled where the boats stopped. Cities that grew up where this happened are called *fall line* cities. Trenton on the Delaware River and Richmond on the James, are fall line cities.

Man has not always been content with Nature's work. He has often dredged, widened, or added canals to rivers to make them more useful. The St. Lawrence Seaway is a good example of this. The seaway is a combination of man-made and natural rivers, locks, lakes, and canals. It makes it possible for large ocean ships to reach the Great Lakes.

SOME PROMINENT RIVERS OF THE WORLD			
Name	Location	Flows into	Length (miles)
Nile	Africa	Mediterranean Sea	4,100
Amazon	South America	Atlantic Ocean	3,900
Mississippi-Missouri	North America	Gulf of Mexico	3,892
Yangtze	Asia	East China Sea	3,400
Ob-Irtysh	Asia	Kara Sea	3,400
Congo	Africa	Atlantic Ocean	2,900
Yellow	Asia	Yellow Sea	2,900
Mackenzie	North America	Arctic Ocean	2,635
La Plata-Paraná	South America	Atlantic Ocean	2,450
Murray-Darling	Australia	Great Australian Bight	2,310
Volga	Europe	Caspian Sea	2,290
Yukon	North America	Bering Sea	1,979
Rio Grande	North America	Gulf of Mexico	1,885
Danube	Europe	Black Sea	1,750

W. B. Hamilton, U.S. Geological Survey

A glacier is a river of ice. Notice how this glacier in Antarctica seems to spill down over the mountains like a river.

Moving Fields of Ice

CHILDREN who like to play in the snow often exclaim, "Oh, I wish the snow would last forever!"

Have you ever wondered what would happen if the snow did not melt? In the polar regions and on some of our very high mountains, much of the snow does last right through the summer. By watching what takes place in these regions we have a chance to find the answer to our question.

The snow that falls there does not stay fluffy like newly fallen snow. It may melt a little on top, but then as colder weather comes, it freezes almost like ice. Each new snowfall piles up more and more snow. Year after year for thousands of years this may repeat itself. And the ice-from-snow layer gets thicker and thicker.

As this ice-snow piles up very high, its own weight causes the ice at the bottom to become *plastic* (have the ability to bend without breaking) and move outward at the edges toward lower ground. It is these slowly moving ice sheets on land that we call glaciers.

43

This is the top of an iceberg. The biggest part of an iceberg is always hidden under water.

Glaciers that form on high mountains move slowly down the valleys toward the foot of the mountains. They may move only a few inches or a few feet a day. When their forward edges get down where the weather is warmer, they melt more rapidly.

There are many glaciers in North America, especially along the mountainous coasts of southern Alaska and northern British Columbia. Other glaciers are in Montana and on such high western peaks as Mount Rainier in Washington and Mount Shasta in California.

Most of the island of Greenland is covered by a huge glacier that has been collecting for many thousands of years. The ice in places is more than 8,000 feet thick. It is higher toward the center, so the ice creeps slowly toward the sea. Huge tongues of this ice push their way into the ocean. They break off in the water and float away from the land in the form of icebergs. Seamen in the North Atlantic must keep a sharp lookout for them, as a collision with an iceberg may sink or seriously damage a ship.

Thousands of years ago large glaciers, much like the ice sheet now on Greenland, moved southward across Canada and much of the United States. Such large glaciers have more than once moved southward and then melted back. At least four of these advances and retreats are known to have occurred.

As these huge ice masses with their tremendous weight moved slowly forward, loose soil and rocks were frozen into the bottom of the ice and carried along. The glaciers, thus shod with hard rocks, acted like a huge rasp or file in wearing away the solid surface rocks over which they were moving. Softer rocks were ground to flour-like particles. Valleys were deepened and broadened. Hills and mountains were carved down, and more and more material was added to the rock load carried by the moving glacier. As the ice melted, this enormous amount of debris, composed of rocks of all shapes and sizes, was left to form irregular hills and obstructions that blocked the flow of water and formed many large basins. These hollows and basins form most of our northern lakes. Many waterfalls, even Niagara, were first formed by great quantities of water from the melting glaciers flowing over the uneven surface of the land.

Even today in the mountains of northwestern Montana, there remain between 80 and 90 glaciers. A section of the state has been set aside as Glacier National Park. There are many glaciers today in the mountains of Alaska and Norway. In fact, all of northern Europe was at one time covered by a huge ice sheet. The little country of Switzerland still has about 1,000, and the fjords of Norway were formed, or at least deepened, by glaciers.

So we see that enough of the fluffy snowflakes packed together into solid sheets of ice form glaciers, and glaciers have made great changes in the surface of the earth.

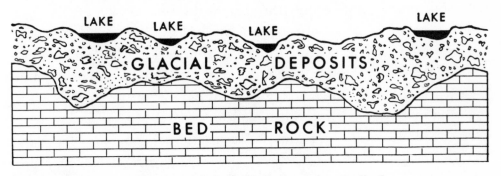

This drawing shows small lake basins, and the irregular distribution of glacial deposits on a bed rock surface.

This is Crater Lake in Oregon.

Joseph Muench

Lakes, Large and Small

O N A WARM summer evening what is more fun than to dive into a crystal clear lake and slice one's way through the cool water! Or perhaps to you a lake suggests a pleasant day of fishing or sailing.

Lakes surely rank along with rivers in their importance to mankind. They are centers of recreation. They provide a source of water supply for numerous towns and cities, for irrigation of land, and even much of the water for many of the rivers themselves. They, too, furnish an important means of inland transportation. They hold back water and reduce floods. For example, there are never any floods on the St. Lawrence River because the Great Lakes act as storage basins which release the water quite evenly throughout the year. Lakes are also the source of a large amount of fresh-water fish.

Lakes are found in nearly all parts of the world. The first requirement in the formation of a lake is that there must be a cup or basin in the earth's surface to catch and hold the water. There are several ways in which these basins are formed.

Most of the lakes in Minnesota, Wisconsin, Michigan, and New York were formed by glaciers. The best known lakes of glacial origin are the Great Lakes—Lakes Superior, Michigan, Huron, Erie, and Ontario. Lake Superior is the world's largest fresh-water lake.

Let us now look at some of the other ways that lakes were formed. There is one in the state of Oregon that is of special interest. Lying as it does in the crater of an old volcano it is rightly called Crater Lake. It is the largest crater lake in the world, being more than 5 miles across, and is known to

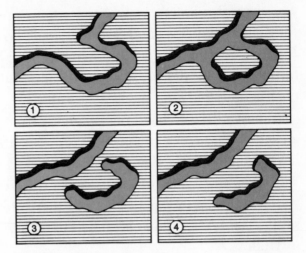

Formation of an oxbow lake.

be about 2,000 feet deep. No rivers flow into it. It is fed entirely by rain and snow that fall directly into the basin.

While we are thinking about Oregon, we may as well look at another kind of lake formation. The Warner Lakes of Oregon were formed by the breaking and slipping of a portion of the earth's crust, the same sort of thing that causes earthquakes. The ground sank enough in places to make basins which filled with water. Several lakes in Tennessee formed after an earthquake shook the lower Mississippi Valley in 1811. There are other lake basins of this type in the United States, in Hungary, in southern Sweden, and in Africa.

Sometimes a river cuts across one of its curves leaving the curve behind. The old curved portion with water standing in it may be walled off from the new stream to form a lake. We call a lake formed in this way, an oxbow lake.

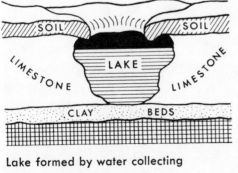

Lake formed by water collecting in a *sink* in limestone rock.

In Kentucky there are hundreds of small lakes that were made by water collecting in *sinks* in the limestone rock of this region. Sinks are holes formed when running water dissolves the limestone so that the surface "sinks" at that point. Usually sinks that

47

contain water are those whose bottoms are below the water table so they are fed by ground water. Small lakes like this occur, too, in Indiana, central Florida, and many other places. Sometimes lakes are formed by landslides, by beaver dams, by lava flows, and by other obstructions that stop the flow of water.

Almost all lakes have one or more streams running into them and an outlet through a stream or river. But there are a few lakes which have no outlets. In that case, the minerals which are carried into the lake over thousands of years remain there because the only loss of water is through evaporation, and the water becomes more and more salty. The best example of this in the United States is Great Salt Lake in Utah.

Since the water in lakes is not moving rapidly, the water usually does not hold large quantities of dirt in it. Many lakes are clear and blue. Eventually, though, they become filled with dirt because rivers and streams carry it in. So probably our present lakes will gradually disappear. Thus, it has been said that rivers are enemies of lakes. But we need not worry about the gradual disappearance of the lakes because it takes a long, long time for lakes to fill. Anyway, new lakes are likely to form wherever nature's many forces make new basins on the earth's surface.

SOME PROMINENT LAKES OF THE WORLD			
Name	Location	Area in square miles	Greatest Depth in feet
Caspian Sea*	Russia-Iran	143,500	3,260
Superior	U.S.A.-Canada	31,800	1,300
Victoria	Africa	26,800	265
Aral Sea*	Russia	25,300	220
Huron	U.S.A.-Canada	23,000	750
Michigan	U.S.A.	22,400	920
Tanganyika	Africa	12,700	4,700
Great Bear Lake	Canada	12,275	1,360
Baykal	Russia	11,800	5,300
Erie	U.S.A.-Canada	9,910	210
Ontario	U.S.A.-Canada	7,600	800

*Despite the name "Sea," these are actually lakes.

The water cycle is the process by which water travels from sea to air to land to sea again, in an endless pattern, as shown above.

Some Wonders of the Sea

AT LEAST three-fourths of the surface of the earth is covered by water. We call the large bodies of water between the continents oceans or seas. The main difference between an ocean and a sea is largely a matter of size and depth. The water in both is salt water. But most people choose to call the largest bodies of salt water, oceans, and the smaller ones, seas. So looking at a globe or a map of the world we find the words, Pacific Ocean, Atlantic Ocean, Indian Ocean, Arctic Ocean. We find, also, Caspian Sea, Bering Sea, Black Sea, and North Sea.

Water tends to flow to the lowest place it can find. As the ocean is lower than the land, when rain and snow and hail fall on the land, some of the water runs off to the ocean through the streams. From the ocean the water evaporates to form clouds again. We call this endless process the *water cycle*.

49

The water that runs into the ocean carries salt and other minerals with it. When the water evaporates, it leaves the salt behind. In this way the ocean continues to get more and more salty. Since ocean water is too salty to drink, ocean-going ships have to carry a supply of fresh water. If all the salt from the ocean were separated from the water and spread out in a layer, it would make a blanket 150 feet deep covering the entire surface of the earth!

The bottom of the ocean is not even and level, although it is more so than most of the land. If all the water could be drained away, we would see that the ocean floor not only had deep valleys but also great ridges of land rising from it. In some places mountains come up above the top of the water to form islands. The average depth of the ocean is a little over 2 miles, but some places are over 6 miles deep. The deepest known point is near the Mariana Islands, where a depth of nearly 7 miles was measured. This is much deeper than the highest mountain is tall.

Many forces are gradually wearing down the land and carrying it into the ocean. Rivers, as they slow down upon entering the ocean, deposit the soil and other sediment they carry, sometimes making deltas, as such formations of land at the mouth of a river are called. Ocean waves lashing and beating against the shore line wear down

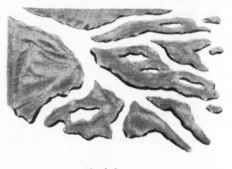

A delta

the coast—even the rocks—in time. Tides and ocean currents are continually scouring the bays and shores. Sometimes there are slight risings or sinkings in the ocean floor itself. Due to all of these things, the shore line of the ocean is gradually changing.

Ocean currents are caused primarily by winds and the unequal heating of the water. Two principal currents near the United States are the Gulf Stream and the North Pacific Current. The Gulf Stream, flowing from the Gulf of Mexico north along the east coast of Florida, is joined by other branches from the south. This huge flow of water several miles wide is like a river within the ocean. It moves at the rate

Not all mountains are on land. Many are under the sea. Some of these undersea mountains are so tall that their peaks rise out of the ocean, forming islands.

of 3 to 5 miles an hour, carrying warm water north and east across the Atlantic to give the British Isles and the coast of Norway a mild climate in spite of their being so far north. The North Pacific Current does the same for our own northwest coast and for that of British Columbia and southeastern Alaska.

Within the oceans exists a tremendous abundance of life. There are thousands of different kinds of fish and other underwater creatures and plants, in an almost unbelievable variety of colors, shapes, and sizes. There are whales that weigh more than 100 tons. There are immense plants that sway in the almost constantly moving water. There

51

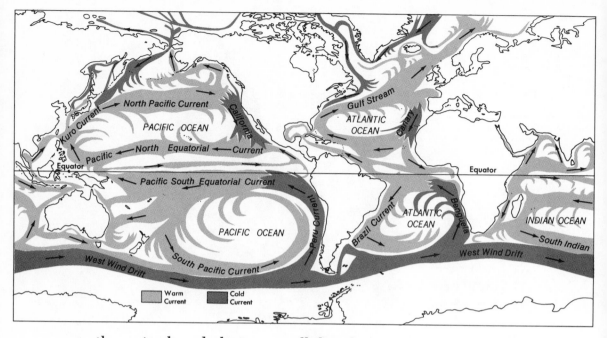

are other animals and plants so small that they can be seen only under a microscope.

The ocean is a fascinating and amazing jungle of strange plants and animals. But because of the tremendous pressure of the water at its lower depths, we cannot explore the deeper parts of the oceans without special equipment. Special types of undersea craft, called *submersibles,* have been built to explore the ocean depths. In one such craft, scientists have descended to the deepest known place in the sea, nearly seven miles below the surface in the Pacific Ocean.

OCEANS OF THE WORLD			
Name	**Area in square miles**	**Greatest Depth (feet)**	**Location of Greatest Depth**
Pacific Ocean	64,186,300	36,198	Near Mariana Islands
Atlantic Ocean	33,420,000	28,374	Near Puerto Rico
Indian Ocean	28,350,500	25,344	Near Java
Arctic Ocean	5,105,700	17,880	Eurasian Basin, near Svalbard
Total	131,062,500		

Note: The area figures for the oceans include all adjoining seas, so that all continuous salt water on earth is included. For example, the Mediterranean Sea area is included in the Atlantic Ocean, and the China Sea is included within the Pacific Ocean.

How Mountains Are Formed

YOU can see how mountains are made by a simple experiment. First, get three packages of gelatin of different colors such as red, green, and yellow. Then dissolve one of them in a cup of hot water and pour it into a small pan about 4 inches deep and 4 or 5 inches wide. After the gelatin has cooled and set, dissolve another package and pour it on top of the first. After this has set, put the third on top of the second and let it set. Now you have three colored layers of gelatin in the pan. Imagine these are layers of rock in the earth's surface.

Let us now proceed with the experiment. Find a thin board just the width of the pan. Carefully push the board downward between the gelatin and one end of the pan. Then push the board firmly and slowly against the gelatin. The gelatin begins to bulge in some spots. Continue to push and watch very carefully. The layers are now pushed into curves. You have made mountains. Most of the real mountains have been made in much the same way.

Whatever happens your

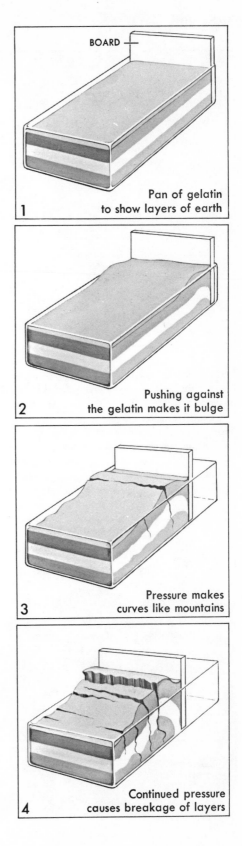

1 Pan of gelatin to show layers of earth

2 Pushing against the gelatin makes it bulge

3 Pressure makes curves like mountains

4 Continued pressure causes breakage of layers

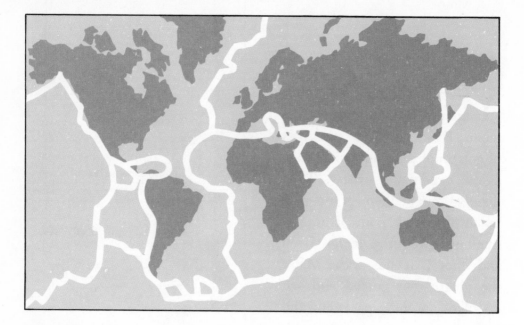

Some scientists think that mountains can be formed by the process of *plate tectonics*. It is thought that the earth's *crust* (outer layer of rock) is divided into several huge sections, or *plates*, as shown on the map (above). The plates slide very slowly over the earth's *mantle*, a lower layer of rock that is heated from the earth's interior. Heat currents in the mantle push the plates against one another, producing tremendous forces that can buckle the material at the edges of the plates to form mountains, as shown in the diagram (below). Usually, one plate is forced underneath the other, and the lower plate is slowly absorbed by the mantle. Where the two plates pass one another, heated rock from the mantle can burst through the crust to form volcanoes. And the movement of the plates against one another can also cause earthquakes.

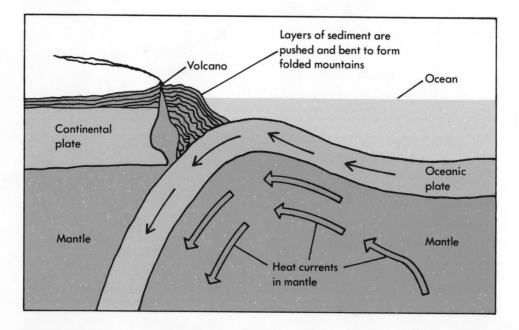

This is Paricutin, the famous Mexican volcano. (See next page)

experiment is a success because the same things happen to real rock layers during the process of mountain building.

If some great force pushed the rocks of the earth the way you pushed the gelatin, the rocks would rise far into the air at each bulging curve. The higher bulges would be the highest ranges of mountains. The lower bulges would be lower ranges of mountains.

You may wonder what great force would be pushing sideways on the rocks of the earth's crust. One way this may occur is shown in the illustrations on the previous page. Mountains formed in this way usually are along coasts or in lines running about the same direction as coastlines. The Appalachians near the eastern coast of the United States were probably formed in this way. Another example is the Sierra Nevada in California. Generally mountains do not stand alone. They are usually parts of a long ridge of mountains called a range.

Mountains are also formed in other ways. While some of the land is raised into folds as we have just described, other areas are raised into high flat lands called plateaus. Water forms streams that run across the plateaus. The streams gradually cut down the rock. Finally, as many huge gorges are made, the plateau becomes rough and ragged. The high points then look like mountains. The Catskill Mountains in New York were formed in this way. Pikes Peak in Colorado was formed by the slow process of streams wearing away a plateau, leaving the harder rock standing out by itself.

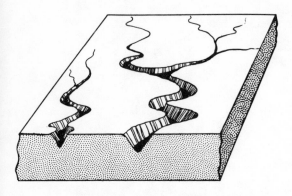

This drawing shows the early effects of erosion on a mountain plateau.

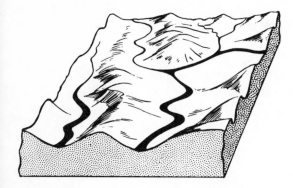

This drawing shows the same plateau in a much later stage of erosion.

There is still a different kind of mountain. In many places over the earth, hot liquid rock called *lava* has oozed out of holes in the ground. Such an opening is called a *volcano*. This lava, along with cinders and ashes blown out by hot gases from within, collected into heaps around the holes and formed cone-shaped hills. As more and more of this hot material was thrown out, the hills became higher and higher until finally they became mountains. The lava gradually cooled and formed hard rock.

Some of the world's highest mountains are volcanic mountains. Mount Aconcagua in Argentina is one. Mount Rainier in Washington is another. The Hawaiian Islands in the Pacific Ocean are really the tops of volcanic mountains. They would be very high if their bases were not so deep in the water.

All the processes that formed mountains in the past are still at work today. But mountains are not often made overnight or in a year. For most of them it has taken millions of years.

There was a case in Mexico, though, some years ago, where a volcano was formed suddenly. Near Paricutin a farmer and his son were plowing in a field when all at once steam and hot ashes began coming out of the ground nearby. Within a few hours hot lava and ashes belched forth and flowed over the countryside destroying plants and trees, and in time even burying a number of villages. For some time before the eruption, the ground where the volcano started had been warmer than at any other place in the area. In the cool evenings picnickers had often gone there to enjoy its warmth. Many of these people must have wondered what made the ground so warm. Imagine their surprise when the earth opened with a rumbling sound and a smoking volcano started to grow.

The United States has several volcanoes that have erupted at times in recent years. One of these is Lassen Peak in northern California. The surrounding region with its hot springs and bubbling mudholes, which tell of intense underground heat, has been set aside as a national park. Other active volcanoes are in Alaska and Hawaii.

Mountains have greatly influenced the lives of people. Certain high ranges cause plenty of rainfall on one side of the mountains and allow the other side little or none. Mountains often serve as boundaries between states and nations. They yield important minerals and precious jewels. They are the source of many streams. They provide scenery and recreation for millions of people.

SOME PROMINENT MOUNTAINS OF THE WORLD		
Name	**Location**	**Height in feet**
Mt. Everest	China-Nepal	29,028
Aconcagua	Argentina	22,835
Mt. McKinley	Alaska	20,320
Mt. Logan	Canada	19,850
Mt. Kilimanjaro	Tanzania	19,340
Orizaba (or Citlaltépetl)	Mexico	18,700
Mt. Elbrus	Russia	18,481
Vinson Massif	Antarctica	16,860
Mont Blanc	France	15,771
Matterhorn	Switzerland-Italy	14,690
Mt. Whitney	California	14,494
Mt. Elbert	Colorado	14,433
Mt. Shasta	California	14,162
Pikes Peak	Colorado	14,110
Mauna Kea	Hawaii	13,680
Fujiyama	Japan	12,389

Bryce Canyon is a wonderland made by erosion.

Rocks and the Stories They Tell

THE solid part of our earth is made of rock. Rocks are found on top of the earth, in the ground, and under the sea. Most of the soil that covers the earth is made of tiny rock particles.

Rocks may be bigger than the Rock of Gibraltar or smaller than a grain of sand. They may be soft or hard, smooth or rough, dull or shiny, heavy or light.

For ages and ages rocks have been changing. Sometimes water wore them smooth. Sometimes great heat melted them until they boiled. Sometimes it became so cold they cracked. Over and over again the forces of wind, water, heat, cold, and pressure have scraped, mixed, melted, shattered, and crushed rocks and changed them into new forms. Water, ice, and wind have carried rocks from one place to another.

Each force that changed a rock left a mark on it. Scientists can read the history of these changes from the marks. They can tell what happened long ago on the earth from the records kept by the rocks.

Most rocks are made of *minerals*. Minerals are usually made of simple substances called *elements*.

Some rocks contain only one mineral. Quartz is this kind of rock.

The two simple substances in quartz are called silicon and oxygen. The billions of shiny glass-like grains in sand are quartz. It is a very abundant mineral. Many everyday things, like glass and sandpaper, are made from quartz.

Most rocks are made of more than one mineral. Granite is this kind of rock. Granite is made of three minerals. They are quartz, feldspar and mica. Some granites contain the mineral, hornblende, instead of mica. The minerals in granite fit together very tightly, and do not crumble apart easily. It is hard for wind and weather to wear away granite. Because of this, people use granite for buildings and monuments that they want to last for a long time. Granite is a good building material.

Metals and valuable stones like diamonds are found in mineral *ore* deposits throughout the world. Ore is a rocky material that must be treated in some way to get the valuable material out of it. Hematite, for instance, is a mineral ore which contains iron. This ore must be heated in hot furnaces to get the iron from it. Pitchblende is a mineral ore which contains uranium. The metal, uranium, is especially valuable today because it is a source of atomic energy.

Here are some precious minerals shown in their natural and polished forms.

DIAMOND

RUBY

SAPPHIRE

TOPAZ

EMERALD

If you were to examine various minerals you would find that some of them are very hard, some quite soft. Surprising as it may seem, graphite, of which the "lead" in your pencil is made, and coal are both composed of the same substance as diamonds. A diamond is the hardest substance known. Graphite is quite soft and greasy, so much so that it is used for making slippery surfaces. There is nothing about the beautiful and precious diamond, which sells for hundreds of dollars a carat, to make one think of coal, which sells for a few dollars a ton, except that they are both made of carbon. The diamond came from bits of carbon which in the earth's processes were crystallized by tremendous and unusual heat and pressure.

Thus we see that the same minerals may be different because of special treatment that they received. Also rocks containing the same minerals may be different because these minerals are mixed in different proportions. As the result of various mixtures and the way they were treated there are many varieties of rock. We can best understand them if we examine the ways in which rocks were formed. There were three principal ways.

Ages ago when the earth was very hot, much of the matter from which rocks are made was melted into a liquid. When the liquid rock cooled, a special kind of rock was formed. These rocks are called *igneous* rocks, meaning "formed by fire."

When sand and sea shells and other particles settle in a body of water, a layer of rock is gradually formed. At the bottom of the ocean sea shells continually collect and, after thousands of years, deep layers of *sedimentary* rocks are made. As portions of the earth's surface have shifted, many of these sedimentary rocks, which once were at the bottom of the sea, are now on land.

Both igneous and sedimentary rocks are sometimes changed by great pressure or heat into another type. In the pushing and sliding of parts of the earth's surface, which make mountains and valleys and cause earthquakes, some rocks get enormous pressure put on them that may change them considerably. The new type of rock formed in this manner is given a big name that means "changed." The name is *metamorphic* rock.

So we have three types of rock: igneous, sedimentary, and meta-

Igneous rock formation—Devil's Tower, Wyoming.

morphic. Granite is one of the most common igneous rocks. It is a very hard rock with a great deal of quartz in it. Lava from volcanoes forms into igneous rock.

A common sedimentary rock is limestone. As it is often formed from sea shells settling to the floor of the ocean and becoming cemented together, most of the limestone is gray in color. It is a fairly soft rock, not difficult to cut, and makes an excellent stone for buildings.

Sandstone is also sedimentary. It is formed by small grains of sand being firmly cemented together. This often happens to sand that settles to the bottom of a stream and remains there over a long period. Another sedimentary rock is shale which is formed by clays and mud settling from water and gradually hardening.

When granite is changed by heat and pressure, the minerals become arranged in streaks or bands and the rock is then called gneiss. When ordinary mud hardens it is called shale. This may be changed by heat and pressure to form slate. Slate is harder than shale and because it breaks into thin sheets it is used for roofing shingles. When limestone is crystallized by heat and pressure, it becomes marble. Gneiss, slate, and marble are examples of metamorphic rocks.

Scientists who study the rocks and from them piece together the history of the earth are called geologists. *Piece together* is what they have to do with the facts they find in order to learn the whole story. For although the layers of rock formed at the different periods con-

Shell Limestone   Granite   Gneiss

tain records of what was happening on the earth at that time, the rocks have been warped and shifted so much that to read them is like reading a book that has been torn and battered and damaged, with some of the pages missing.

It is in the sedimentary rocks that we get most of our information about the earth's history. Sea animals died and their bodies sank to the bottom of the ocean. Rivers and floods washed huge loads of sediment into the ocean and into lakes, carrying with it the bodies or skeletons of land animals that also settled into the mud. As the layers of limestone and shale and sandstone were formed, they held embedded in them these fossils, or remains, of the life of that particular period.

The oldest rocks are largely igneous, and no evidence of life appears in them. The very old sedimentary rocks also show nothing, but the earliest forms of life were doubtless small and soft and easily destroyed. However, as living things developed bones and shells of hard material, they began to leave a permanent record behind them. As layer after layer of rock was built, traces were left of the more advanced forms, fossils of ferns, skeletons of fish, amphibians, reptiles—some of them huge monsters—animals, and plants, similar to those we have today. We can follow the development of life by studying the rocks.

All of those records remain for man to study and to ponder over. As we said before, they often are mixed up but many times nature's processes have helped us by making the pages and the stories they tell easier to find. Upheavals in the earth's crust have placed large areas that were once under water, high and dry. Running water has cut deep canyons, leaving the layers of rock exposed.

This picture shows a fossil embedded in limestone.

How Water Carves Caves and Canyons

MILLIONS of years ago a stream began cutting a channel for itself. At that time the stream was unnamed, and so were the mountains in which it had its source. Day by day and little by little through the ages, it continued its work. Its chief tools were the bits of sand and gravel it carried in its moving water, and its helpers were the rains and snows of the mountains.

The stream had to make its way for the most part over layers of very old rock. Some of these layers were soft and some were very hard. But once a valley is cut below the water table and gains a permanent stream, the wearing away continues even through the hardest rock. In time deep gorges were developed. Today that stream which began in a small gulley is known as the Colorado River, and the steep cliffs cut by the stream form the walls of the famous Grand Canyon.

The work of the Colorado River is by no means completed. Aided by the action of rains, frost, winds, and landslides, it is still wearing away rock, and will continue to do so for many years to come. At present the brim in many places is over a mile above the stream, and the canyon 10 or 12 miles across and nearly 300 miles long.

Part of the wonder of the Grand Canyon lies in the many-colored rocks, whose varied tints range from white to deep red. As the sun moves across the sky bringing sunshine and shadow to different parts of the canyon, the visitor is held spellbound by the remarkable play of colors on the rough cliffs that make up its gigantic walls.

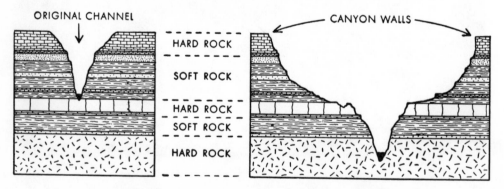

Formation of a canyon such as the Grand Canyon.

Idaho State Board of Publicity

Snake River Canyon

Tributaries also have carved their way down through the colored rocks to join the Colorado on its way to the sea. No wonder the river itself is red with ground-up red rock through which it eats its way. Thus, it is not strange that the Spanish explorers named it the Colorado—the color of red.

Many rivers have carved deep canyons. The Snake River, which empties into the Columbia, has cut the deepest canyon in the United States where it flows between the boundaries of Idaho and Oregon. This remarkable gorge averages 5,500 feet in depth for a distance of 40 miles. The Yellowstone River in Wyoming and the Yakima River in Washington also have carved deep gorges. All these are amazing examples of what swift water can do. The towering walls remain as magnificent monuments to the rivers' ceaseless efforts.

The formation of caves is as wonderful as that of canyons. Here again, water is the sculptor, this time carving rugged chambers out of

65

This picture shows the steep cliffs and beautiful colors of the Grand Canyon.

rock lying beneath the earth's surface. In its journey underground the water gathers up quantities of animal and vegetable matter. This matter, in combination with the water, forms carbonic acid which dissolves certain substances in rock. The rock most easily dissolved by this solution of water and acid is limestone. That is why the most remarkable caves in the world are found in limestone regions.

Limestone rock occurs in layers, sometimes several layers resting on top of each other. Rain water seeps through any small cracks and dissolves some of the rock as it runs along. As the space under the ground gets bigger and bigger, the roof over the hole may fall in, forming a sink.

If, however, the roof does not fall in as the hole grows larger, then the hole becomes a cave. Water sometimes eats its way through the rock and creates a network of caverns.

Usually the water that has trickled through the rock collects to form an underground stream. As the stream gets larger, it cuts its way lower into the rock and runs away to become a part of a surface stream outside the cave. Sometimes no stream can be seen in the floor of the cave, although one seems to be flowing out of the cave. Such a stream is called a *lost river*. In reality, such a river is running along in the cracks and layers of rock below the floor of the cave.

Many of the large caves are famous for beautiful rock formations, which have the appearance of huge icicles hanging from the ceilings, and for the cone and needle-like shapes of the same material standing on their floors. These formations are called *stalactites* and *stalagmites*. The stalactites grow down from the ceiling and the stalagmites grow up from the floor.

Who ever heard of rocks growing? But that is just what these "icicles" of rock do, only in a special way. The water which comes trickling through the ground above the cave roof passes through the limestone rock. Upon reaching the ceiling of the cave, it begins a drop by drop journey to the water table. In so doing, it comes in contact with the air moving in the cave, which causes some of the water to evaporate. When the water evaporates, it cannot take the dissolved rock substance with it into the air. So it deposits the whitish material on the cave roof. This deposit is the beginning of a stalactite. Once a stalactite is started it keeps on growing just as a real icicle does.

Not all the water, however, evaporates from the ceiling. Some of it drips to the cave floor. Here, too, some of the water is evaporated, and again a mite of rock substance is left behind; this time on the floor. Thus a stalagmite grows up from the floor. Hundreds of these stalactites and stalagmites may be formed in a huge cave. When such a cavern is lighted, it looks like a fairyland palace of dazzling

Hillus and Matthis

Stalactites are deposits that hang from the roofs of caves.

Hillus and Matthis

Stalagmites are deposits formed on the floors of caves.

white columns and immense stony needles.

Sometimes the water contains other minerals besides lime. These minerals produce the beautiful streaks of color which appear in the stalactites and stalagmites in some caverns and caves.

Every year thousands of travelers visit caves found in the United States. Although every state has some caves, they are found in greater numbers in Kentucky, Tennessee, southern Indiana, Virginia, northern Florida and New Mexico.

Mammoth Cave, Kentucky, is one of the largest caves. Here a single underground passage is more than eight miles long. Connecting shafts make it possible to travel 150 miles through its various caverns and passageways.

Part of a regular tour for visitors is a boat trip on an underground river. There one may see fish and other creatures, such as crayfish and beetles, that are entirely blind. Their ancestors lived in this dark underground region so long that they lost the use of their eyes.

Carlsbad Cavern, in New Mexico, is the world's largest known cave. It goes down to a depth of more than 1,300 feet. One of its rooms is nearly a mile long and more than 600 feet wide.

What Makes an Earthquake?

A N EARTHQUAKE is a sudden movement or quaking of the earth. Thousands of earthquakes take place every year. Most of them do no harm because they are small or happen under the sea. Some earthquakes, however, are very destructive. Whole cities may be destroyed and many people killed.

What makes an earthquake? Before people knew anything about the cause of earthquakes, they blamed them on animals which live under the earth or water. In India people believed a mole caused the earth to shake. In South America they blamed a whale. In Japan they thought a catfish was responsible.

Although all scientists agree that animals do not cause earthquakes, they do not always agree on what does cause them. They do know that there are powerful forces at work inside the earth. These forces cause underground pressure and movement. Movement and pressure build up tension and trap energy in the rocky layers on the surface and inside the earth. When the pressure becomes too great the rock snaps and makes a deep crack called a *fault*. At the same time, all the stored-up tension and energy is released. When this happens there is an earthquake. Some earthquakes happen when a fresh break, or fault, is formed. Others occur when the sides along an old fault suddenly slip. The sides of a fault may actually jump when this happens. They may jump up, down, or sideways. A great earthquake in Alaska lifted a part of the sea floor near the coast almost 50 feet.

An earthquake releases tremendous amounts of energy, which is sent out as waves through the rocks of the earth's crust and interior. Much of this energy is driven deep within the earth, but the rest can cause severe damage on the earth's surface. Buildings can be shaken down, underground pipes broken, and bridges smashed.

Earthquakes happen most often where parts of the earth's crust are pushing against one another. One of these areas is located along the west coast of the United States. Like most earthquake areas, it has well-known faults. One of the most famous is called the San Andreas Fault. This great crack in the earth's crust is 500 miles long. It runs

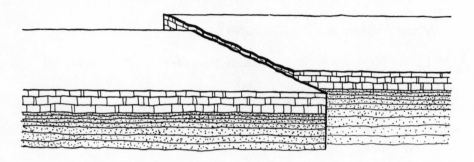

This drawing shows a strike fault or side movement of rock layers.

across California, the long way, and extends deep into Mexico. Faults are not always in plain sight, but there are many places along the San Andreas Fault where deep cracks show on the surface.

This fault has caused many severe earthquakes. One of them was the great San Francisco earthquake of 1906. Some San Franciscans call this famous disaster the San Francisco "fire" because of the terrible fire that followed the earthquake.

Fires are a great danger to a city hit by an earthquake. The first shock waves can break underground waterpipes and start fires at the same time. Without water, firemen are helpless to control the flames. Many cities near earthquake areas store water above the ground for this reason.

When earthquakes occur on the floor of the ocean, powerful shock

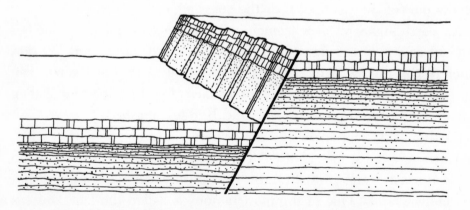

This drawing shows a gravity fault or vertical movement of rock layers.

Almost every link of a concrete bridge in Japan was destroyed by an earthquake.

waves are sent out through the water at speeds of about 500 miles per hour. In 1946, an underwater earthquake near the Aleutian Islands, off the coast of Alaska, sent out waves that became 40 feet high when they reached shallow coastal waters. These waves were powerful enough to cause considerable damage and the loss of over 200 lives at Hilo, Hawaii, 2,300 miles away.

One of the worst earthquakes on record occurred in the Tokyo area of Japan in 1923 in which more than 140,000 people lost their lives. There, too, some of the damage and loss of life was caused by the huge waves that rolled in from the sea.

Fortunately many earthquakes are so slight that they are never felt. In fact, small earthquakes take place almost every day in some part of the world. Scientists have devised an instrument called a *seismograph* which keeps a record of them.

This is the way the seismograph works. If you hold a pencil lightly on a piece of paper with one hand and pull the paper straight forward with the other hand, you draw a straight line on the paper. But if you pull the paper forward and wiggle it sideways, too, then you get

71

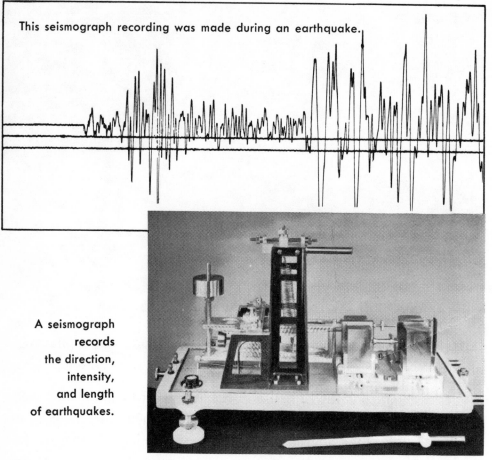

This seismograph recording was made during an earthquake.

A seismograph records the direction, intensity, and length of earthquakes.

U.S. Department of Commerce, Coast and Geodetic Survey

a crooked line. The more you wiggle the paper the more crooked the line becomes.

The base of a seismograph, containing a slowly moving roll of paper, is fastened to the deep bed rock of the earth so that it shakes whenever the crust of the earth shakes. A pencil or some marking device suspended above traces a line on the paper. Whenever a crooked line appears, it means the bed rock has been shaken. A seismograph even registers tremors that are too faint to be felt by people.

Man cannot control the forces in the earth's crust. However, we should not fear future earthquakes. Serious ones very seldom occur. Moreover, well-built buildings are not usually damaged much by earthquakes.

Protecting Our Resources

WHEN the white settlers first began moving westward across the United States, they were amazed by the richness of the country. They moved so slowly on foot, on horseback, or by wagon, that the great forests which stretched out across the eastern part of the country seemed endless. Wild life was plentiful. The streams and lakes were full of fish. Coming at last to mile after mile of prairie land, they were delighted with the rich soil they found when they turned up the thick sod with their plows.

The idea grew in men's minds that the new land was filled with unlimited treasure; that there was more natural wealth than could ever be used. So when the pioneers wanted to clear land for farming, they burned away the trees. If the fire got out of control and swept for miles, they did not care. When they wanted buffalo hides, they killed the buffaloes and stripped off their skins, often leaving the meat to rot on the ground. When the fish in a lake became scarce, the fishermen moved on to another lake.

Little by little, as more and more people spread across the country,

U.S. Department of Commerce, Coast and Geodetic Survey

Unwise use of land can change fertile grassland into wind-swept sandy dunes.

the results of this terrible waste became clear. Wild turkeys, once abundant, became fewer and fewer. The great herds of buffalo dwindled until there were only a few animals left. Mines that had been improperly developed in order to remove the richest parts first, caved in and flooded, preventing further work. Pasture land was often ruined by allowing too many cattle to graze on it.

Some of the people who caused this terrible waste were careless; others were ignorant. Many did not realize that by destroying the trees and plants, they were destroying the animals, too. All forest animals depend directly or indirectly on the forest for food. If all the trees in a forest are cut down, the food supply is destroyed and the animals die.

Tree and grass roots hold a lot of water in the ground. This underground water feeds streams and rivers. If the trees and grass are taken away, water does not collect in the ground, and the streams dry up. Without water, fish and other wild life die.

Fortunately, about 60 years ago, some people began to realize that this waste must stop. Theodore Roosevelt was among the first to awaken the country to this need. Laws were passed and a national program was begun to save our country's natural wealth.

As people learned the importance of conserving our resources and the best ways to conserve them, the land was renewed and improved in many ways. The supply of fish and other wild life was built up by careful restocking and by protective laws. Forests were replanted so that by careful use they would continue to fill our needs. People began to use soil more wisely.

Soil is probably our greatest single wealth. Where it is worn away completely, new soil may never form. Luckily, there are ways to prevent the wearing away, or *erosion,* of soil. Wise farmers know

Both of these pictures show land in the state of Iowa. In the upper half, an Iowa conservation worker looks at the waste caused by plowing in straight rows. The lower half shows the rich look of land where curved contour plowing has stopped erosion.

EROSION

CONTOUR FARMING

that plowing the same fields for years and years causes erosion. They know fields need a rest from the plow. When this happens they often grow soil-binding plants like grass to rebuild the land.

Farmers who grow crops on hilly land, where the water runs down-hill rapidly know that rain water will carry away soil faster than any other force. They plow around the hills and curves in the land, instead of straight up-and-down. This is called *contour* farming. When this is done every furrow becomes a pocket to catch rain, instead of a downhill path for the rain to carry away the soil.

The government has done and is doing many things to help save our natural resources. It has helped farmers learn methods like the ones that prevent soil erosion. It saved huge areas, rich in natural resources, and made these our national parks. It set up forest ranger stations to guard our forests from fires. It created the Department of Health, Education, and Welfare to protect our people.

For conservation means more than the protection of our natural resources, it means the protection of people, or human resources, too. Have you ever stopped to think that just by taking care of

This kind of waste can be prevented.

Wisconsin Conservation Department

What can you do to help conserve our resources? You can be careful with campfires like the campers in the picture below.

This lookout tower is used to help forest rangers spot fires. Do you see the little square house about halfway up the tower? The forest ranger lives there.

yourself, you are conserving human resources?

Many private groups and people outside of the government are interested in conservation. Some of these groups are for boys and girls. You may be a member of a 4 H Club or belong to the Boy Scouts or the Girl Scouts. If you do, you know that conservation is part of the work these groups do.

All this work has improved our country greatly, but there is still much work to do. For, if the United States is to keep its important place in world leadership, each one of us must do all he can to protect both our natural and human resources.

How the Weather Affects Us All

YOU wake up some morning and it is raining. If the skies have been clear for several days and you have not read the late weather forecast, you are quite surprised at the change. If you are planning to do something out-of-doors, you are disappointed. Something has happened to the weather. Perhaps your program for the day or some part of it has to be changed.

A successful picnic or outing at the beach requires fair weather. The farmer needs a certain amount of sunshine and rain during his growing season but prefers very dry weather when he is ready to harvest his crops. Boaters and airplane pilots hope for good weather, since they could be in serious trouble if a storm occurred unexpectedly.

In the earliest times people looked to the heavenly bodies as the givers of all things good and bad, including the weather. Of course, they were right about the sun making our weather. It does so more fully than they could have realized. But no important influence on the earth by the planets or stars has ever been found.

People also used to watch certain signs in nature to tell what the weather was going to be like. If in the fall the animals seemed to be getting an extra heavy coat of fur, the people thought it meant that a

Weather

very cold winter was on the way. There were many such beliefs that were based largely on guesswork or superstition.

Gradually other signs were discovered that really did have a great deal of truth to them. Before storms, sounds could be heard at a greater distance. If in hot weather a pitcher of cold water gathered many beads of water like perspiration on the outside, people said rain was coming. Signs like these do tell us something about the weather. They indicate that the air has a lot of moisture in it.

The noted Italian scientist Galileo was the first to make an exact science of the study of weather. One of the important things he did was to invent the thermometer. Although the thermometer can *record* temperatures, it cannot show what weather may be on the way. In 1643 Torricelli, a pupil of Galileo, invented the barometer, an important instrument in *predicting* the weather.

The barometer helps tell what kind of weather is coming by showing how light or heavy the air is. Because a change in the weight of the air, or *atmospheric pressure*, is a sign of changing weather, the barometer is one of the chief tools used in forecasting the weather. The approach of lighter, or lower-pressure, air is indicated by a "falling" barometer. A low-pressure system generally brings storms. A "rising" barometer tells of an approaching high-pressure air system and, usually, fair weather.

However, there are other things which act on the weather which the barometer does not record. The modern weatherman has an expert knowledge of what makes weather and relies on a wide variety of instruments to carry on his work. One of his newest tools is the weather satellite. These satellites are now whirling in orbit around the earth, taking photographs of the earth. These photographs give us a broad picture of weather movements around the world.

We are familiar with the daily forecasts of the weather bureau because they are readily available in the newspapers and on television and radio.

The three basic elements which create weather may be listed as heat, moisture, and wind. Weather is heat, moisture, and wind, combined. Let's find out more about the three great weather-makers, beginning with heat.

All four of these weather instruments help people forecast the weather. The one at the top left, is a weather balloon. The little box hanging from the balloon contains instruments and a radio. At the top right, is a weather satellite. This is one of the newest instruments. It is sometimes used to locate hurricanes. At the bottom left, is an anemometer and wind vane. The anemometer measures the speed of the wind. The wind vane shows the direction of the wind. The instrument at the bottom right, is a barometer. It measures air pressure.

Heat and Sunlight

WHEN you walk barefooted on a hot sandy beach, your feet feel hot. This is because of the heat in the sand. Where does the heat come from? From the sun, of course. The sun gives all the heat for all the weather in the world.

Generally speaking, the weather is hot when a considerable amount of sunlight makes it so. The weather is cold when there is little sunlight.

We have already seen in the section *Earth and Sky* how the temperature varies during the day, because of the angle from which we receive the sun's rays. Also, we have read how the angle at which sunlight comes to us is responsible for the seasons of the year.

There is something else that makes it hot in the summer, and cold in the winter. It is the amount of time the sun shines each day. In the summer, days are long. The sun shines strongly for many hours each day. This helps make the weather hot. In the winter, days are short. The sun's rays are weaker than they are in the summer, and there are fewer hours of sunlight. This helps make the weather cold.

Without heat and sunlight we could not live on the earth. Plants would not grow. The earth would be a cold, barren planet.

Even though the sun is our friend, we must be careful not to work or play too long on a hot summer day. Too much sun can cause severe burns or even sunstroke. Too much sun is harmful to many plants, too.

The Wind and Its Work

ANY BOY or girl who has ever flown a kite or watched a windmill turning in the breeze knows some of the things that the wind can do. Did you ever wonder what causes the wind? It is mainly the sun.

Even though the sun may not be shining where we are, it is always shining in many places over the earth. Where the sun shines it heats up the land and the air over it. Warm air, being lighter than cold air, rises. Where the air rises, cooler air around it rushes in to take its place. At the shore of a large body of water we often feel a cool breeze coming in off the water during a hot, sunny day. The cool air is taking the place of the warmer air that is rising above the land. Then at night the land cools off faster than the water so that the breeze usually goes the other way.

These differences in the way the sun warms the air in numerous places help to keep the air moving most of the time. We have upward and downward currents of air which we do not notice unless we happen to be flying in an airplane; and we have the movements of air along the surface of the earth which we call wind.

Sometimes these air movements are mild and cover just a small

83

EXAMPLES OF WIND FORCE AT DIFFERENT VELOCITIES*

LIGHT
(1 to 7 miles per hour)

Slow smoke drift. Wind felt on face. Leaves rustle.

GENTLE
(8 to 12 miles per hour)

Flag waves. Leaves and small twigs in constant motion.

MODERATE
(13 to 18 miles per hour)

Raises dust and loose paper Small branches sway.

FRESH
(19 to 24 miles per hour)

Small trees start to sway. Crested waves form on lakes.

STRONG
(25 to 38 miles per hour)

Whole trees in motion. Umbrellas used with much difficulty.

GALE
(39 to 75 miles per hour)

Great difficulty in walking. Trees uprooted. Buildings damaged.

*Adapted from Beaufort Scale of Wind Force

area, but more often they are part of a large movement of air covering hundreds of miles.

We cannot see the wind, but we can feel the effects of it. We can see dust and other objects that it carries. We can see a flag waving in the breeze and wet clothes on a line being whipped back and forth by it. We can see tree leaves shaking and branches swaying. We can see a hat blowing down the street, and we know that it was the wind that took it off the owner's head.

Perhaps few people have ever stopped to think how many useful things the wind does for us. The wind brings our changes of weather. It brings us rain to water our gardens and farms, and it blows the clouds away to give us sunshine again. It scatters seeds far and wide so that plants grow in new places. In summer it helps to keep us cool. It makes waves on the water and dries our wet bathing suits. It turns windmills. It sails boats. In the days before steam engines were invented, people depended on sailing vessels to make long journeys by water. Columbus could not have discovered America if there had been no wind to push the sails on his ships.

But the wind at times can make us quite uncomfortable and can do

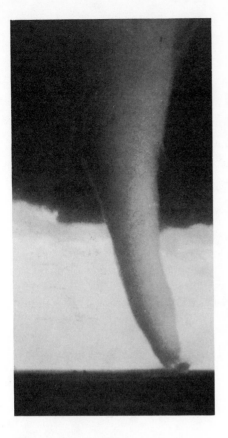

This picture shows the funnel-shaped cloud of a tornado.

much damage. When the air is cold, the wind makes it feel still colder. Wind sometimes causes shipwrecks. It blows away the rich topsoil from the land. It fans forest fires, and often causes big areas of timber to be destroyed before the fire can be controlled.

In the central part of the United States, occasionally there appears a twister or whirlwind which is often called a cyclone, although its correct name is tornado. During a tornado, which has a black funnel-shaped cloud at its center, houses and even people are sometimes picked up and carried blocks away. Thunderstorms without this violent whirlwind center are quite common, but such storms usually are not very destructive.

Lynn Pelham from Rapho Guillumette

This picture, taken from an airplane, shows clouds whirling around the calm center or "eye" of a hurricane. The sun is shining through the clear eye.

The wind makes the sand dunes shift and form patterns like these.

On some parts of the earth, there are occasionally severe storms during which the wind is very strong, even blowing at the rate of one hundred miles or more an hour. In the southeastern part of the United States and in the West Indies a storm like this is called a hurricane.

In the region around the coast of China the same type of storm is called a typhoon.

Winds are continually making changes on the surface of the earth. Next to running water, wind is the greatest force in moving soil. It cuts down hills, the sand that it carries scouring and helping to wear away the rocks. It fills in some valleys and deepens others. Sometimes on the shore of a large body of water the wind piles up big hills of sand called sand dunes.

The sands of the deserts are shifting all the time. In the Gobi desert, in Asia, there are ancient cities which lie buried under heaps of sand piled up over them by the wind.

Moisture in the Air

IF ALL the moisture in the air suddenly became rain it would cover the whole world with an inch of water! Ordinarily, people do not think about all the water stored in the air because they cannot see it.

Sometimes the moisture in the air changes into something we can see like rain, snow, or hail. Sometimes it changes into dew or frost. It changes into fog and clouds, too.

Rain, snow, hail, dew, frost, clouds, and fog are alike in some ways. They are all related to the weather, and they are all made of water. The water in rain, dew, fog, and clouds is liquid. The water in hail is ice. The water in snow and frost is in the form of crystals. If you think about it you will realize that water has a great deal to do with the weather.

Frost sometimes makes beautiful patterns like these on windows.

Even on a clear, dry day there is some water in the air. We cannot see this water because it is in the form of a gas. This gas is called *water vapor.*

All air contains water vapor. It is a very important gas. Without it there would be no plants or animals or people on the earth. There would be no life at all.

Water changes into water vapor when it dries up or *evaporates.* Heat helps water evaporate. You have seen the sun dry up rain puddles. It is the sun's heat that helps the water evaporate and change into water vapor.

There is water vapor in the air around you right now. You can prove it with an experiment.

Fill a jar with ice cubes and put a cover on it. Be sure the outside is dry. Watch the dry surface of the jar closely. Soon you will see tiny drops of water form there. Where do the drops come from? They come from water vapor in the air near the jar. When water vapor cools it forms into little drops of water.

In your experiment you saw how the drops formed on the cool jar. The little drops of water called dew are made the same way. Dew collects on cool ground and plants. You probably have seen dewdrops sparkle on the ground and grass in the morning.

Sometimes the water vapor in air near the ground freezes as it forms. Then tiny crystals called frost form on the ground and plants.

Dew and frost happen close to the ground. Clouds, rain, and snow are made from water vapor high in the air. But how does water vapor get as high as a cloud? The sun's heat warms the air. The warmed air becomes lighter and lighter and rises. Water vapor is part of the air. When the air gets light and rises, the water vapor rises, too.

The water vapor is warm when it begins to rise, but it cools when it gets up high. Billions of tiny droplets form around specks of dust. This makes a cloud. A cloud is really a fog high up in the air. If you have ever been inside a fog, you know what it's like to be inside a cloud.

Some clouds, like the ones called thunderclouds, bring rain. Other clouds never bring rain. Something must happen before the tiny water drops in a cloud can become raindrops. Scientists are not exactly certain how this happens. They do know there is a lot of activity in a cloud that makes raindrops. A thundercloud is really a big snowstorm in the sky. All the rain that falls from it was once snow. The snow melts and turns into raindrops on its way to the ground.

Hail is a kind of frozen rain. It is formed in an interesting way. Raindrops start to fall from the clouds. Then upward gusts of wind blow them back into the clouds. Up and down the raindrops go, and all the time the cold air is freezing them. Finally they leave the clouds in the form of frozen balls of ice.

Winston Pote from Shostal

This beautiful picture of cirrus clouds was taken at sunset. Cirrus means "curl." Can you see how the clouds got their name? If you see clouds like these moving swiftly across the sky you can be fairly certain that bad weather is on the way.

There are many different kinds of clouds. *Cumulus* clouds are the kind that look like huge pieces of cotton floating in the blue sky. Cumulus means "heap." These are fair-weather clouds. When you see them you can expect the day to be bright and fair.

Cirrus clouds ride very high in the sky where it is cold. Cirrus means "curl." These clouds are made of tiny ice crystals. When you see cirrus clouds you can expect a change in the weather, especially if they come after several fair days.

Stratus clouds ride very close to the earth. Stratus means "layer." When these clouds pile on top of one another they look like a layer cake. When they are strung out across the sky they look like pulled taffy. When stratus clouds follow cirrus clouds it is almost certain to rain or snow.

Nimbus clouds almost always bring rain. Nimbus means "rainstorm." They are dark and heavy-looking. The darker the cloud, the larger the drops will be when the rain falls. Nimbus clouds sometimes bring a hard, heavy rain that does not last long.

You may see two kinds of clouds in the sky at the same time. This is not unusual because the clouds are always changing.

Hammond from Frederic Lewis

These are nimbus clouds. When you look up at the sky at clouds like these you know it is time to go inside!

U.S. Geological Survey

These are fair-weather cumulus clouds. Each cloud is at the top of a neck of warm air.

Philip Gendreau, Press Illustration Service

These are stratus clouds. Sometimes stratus clouds are so close to the ground that we walk right through them! Then we call them fog.

91

Scientists do not know what makes lightning, but they do know that it is a huge electric spark. They know that it builds up in clouds called thunderheads. Wild winds blow rain and snow upwards and downwards in these clouds. This makes the electricity build up until there is too much of it to stay in the cloud. When this happens the lightning jumps. It may jump from one cloud to another or it may jump to the ground.

Thunder is the noise the air makes when lightning strikes. Thunder is not dangerous but lightning can be.

Do you know that lightning helps plants grow? All plants must have a gas called nitrogen to live. There is plenty of nitrogen in air, but it must get into the ground before plants can use it. When lightning shoots through the air it changes some of the nitrogen so that it becomes part of the falling rain. Then plants, like the cactus in this picture, can take the nitrogen in through their roots.

Ray Manley from Shostal

August Upitis from Shostal

Snowflakes and Ice

CHILDREN who live where snow never falls or where the ponds and lakes never freeze miss some very exciting adventures. Snow battles, ice skating, and sleigh-ride parties are some of the sports that children in the North look forward to every winter.

Snowflakes are several ice crystals that have joined together. In winter, the water vapor in the cold clouds has turned into ice crystals instead of rain. As in the formation of raindrops, ice crystals fasten onto dust specks. One crystal fastens to another and, when many of them are joined together, they become a snowflake and are heavy enough to fall from the cloud.

The snowflake usually stays frozen when it hits the earth, because the air around the earth is cold in winter.

Sometimes, though, snowflakes melt or are broken on their way down to earth.

We see crystals every day when we look at salt or sugar, but ice crystals are different. They are not smooth and solid like sugar or salt. Ice crystals have six sides and are in beautiful star shapes and flower designs.

No two crystals exactly alike have ever been found. One must look at snow crystals through a magnifying glass in order to see the delicate patterns clearly.

As the soft snowflakes come down to the earth and pile on top of others, some air is left between them so that all outdoors looks as though it were covered with a fluffy white blanket. We look at it and think we have never seen a more beautiful sight. But this beautiful snow can become quite a nuisance, too. Often the wind blows it into huge drifts that block highways and railroad tracks so that they have to be opened by snowplows. Sometimes snow and ice break down telephone lines and trees. Snow on a roof may get so heavy that the roof caves in.

In some parts of the country, as in Minnesota and the Dakotas, such severe blizzards sometimes occur that people have to be careful not to get lost in them.

Traffic practically stops at these times and schools close for a day or two until the storm is over.

When the temperature of the air gets down below 32 degrees, the top layer of water in ponds and lakes begins to freeze into ice crystals. The crystals are somewhat like those that are formed in snow clouds and they have six sides. These stick together and make a coat of ice that floats on top of the water. The ice coat gets thicker as the cold weather continues. The ice always freezes from the top down. When the ice on a pond has frozen far enough down so that it will hold the weight of several people, it is usually safe for ice skating.

Winter gives the plants and many of the animals a rest. Snow helps to keep the earth warm and filled with moisture. It is good for the plants that are buried underneath.

In the spring when the snow melts, some of it soaks into the earth and some of it flows into streams to provide water for fish, for boats, and for many other uses.

Controlling the Weather

A S PEOPLE learned more about the weather, they began to think how nice it would be to always have just the kind of weather they wanted. Many problems must be solved before we can do very much about controlling the weather, but scientists understand enough today to be able to control rain, hail, and frost to a small extent.

It has been discovered that dropping small pieces of dry ice into clouds will sometimes make it rain. The dry ice causes the cloud's tiny droplets of water to join and make larger droplets. When the drops become heavy enough they fall as rain. This is called *seeding* the clouds and is usually done from an airplane. At present, seeding is too costly to be used very much.

As early as the seventeenth century, a way of preventing hail was known. When a cannon is fired into the sky, the shock waves interfere with the air currents that help form hailstones. This prevents hailstones from forming. The shock of a bursting rocket has the same effect. But this method is like seeding the clouds. It is too expensive to be practical.

Probably our most successful venture in controlling the weather

This man is concerned about the freezing effects of frost on his orange
crop. He will stay up all night if necessary to keep the fires burning, and
to check the oranges as he is doing in this picture.

involves the prevention of frost. This is fortunate because frost can
ruin some crops.

Different ways are used to protect different crops. Plants that
grow close to the ground are often covered with straw. Fires or
heaters are used in fruit orchards. They produce a blanket of warm
air that helps keep the frost away.

The oily fuel that was used in smudge pots is no longer allowed in
many places because it made the air too smoky. Modern orchard
heaters burn cleaner fuel, and produce very little smoke.

Climate

THE weather is never the same all over the world. While one area is having rain, another may be having sunshine. Some areas are much warmer than others. In parts of the world where the sun is more directly overhead the climate is warmer than in places where the sun does not climb as high in the sky.

Climate is the word we use to express the usual or average kind of weather for an area. If the temperature is usually high, we say that the climate is hot. If there is usually much rain, we say that such a place has a wet or rainy climate.

The hottest weather on record occurred in El Azizia, Libya, in September, 1922, when the temperature reached 136 degrees. The coldest weather occurred at Vostok, Antarctica, in August of 1960. The temperature was 127 degrees below zero. Possibly the wettest climate in the world is on the island of Kauai, Hawaii. One of the world's driest climates is in South America at Arica, Chile.

Temperature, of course, depends mainly but not entirely on the season or the distance from the equator. Sometimes there are other things that influence temperature a great deal. For instance, high mountain peaks can be very cold even in the tropics. On the other hand, the coast of northern Norway has a fairly mild climate, even though it is quite near the North Pole, because the warm waters of the Gulf Stream come close to its shores.

There are sometimes dry regions not far from places that have a heavy rainfall. This may be due to mountain ranges in between. Western Washington has a great deal of rain because, as the rain clouds blow in from the ocean, they are forced up high above the Cascade Mountains. This cools the clouds and causes the rain to fall. The clouds that do move on have lost most of their moisture, and the land to the east of the mountains gets very little rain. Here the farmers have to irrigate the land in order to raise crops.

Quito, the capital of Ecuador in South America, has the most even temperature of any city in the world. Although it is only fifteen miles from the equator, it is over nine thousand feet above sea level

As the clouds travel up over the mountain they lose their moisture on the way. This makes for a wet climate on one side, and a dry climate on the other side.

which gives its temperature such an even balance that it is always like spring there. Its warmest month averages only about one degree warmer than it coldest. On the other hand, Bismarck, the capital of North Dakota, has a wide variety of temperatures. It has been known to get as cold as 45 degrees below zero there and as hot as 114 degrees above, a difference of 159 degrees.

In most of the lowlands of the hot belt near the equator, winter and summer are much the same. It is always hot. Therefore, the people there do not have much change of seasons. In most of these hot lowlands there is a wet and a dry season, or perhaps a wet season and one not quite so wet, because there is always plenty of rain.

Near the North and South Poles there are two or three months of summer when the sun stays in the sky both day and night, and there is an equal time in the winter when the sun does not shine at all. Except in the short summer, the weather is very cold and nothing can grow except a little moss.

Climate influences the life of every living thing—animals and plants as well as people. In the winter some birds that live in the North migrate, or make long journeys to warmer lands. Many plants cannot live except in a warm climate and few can survive without a fair amount of rainfall. The only land animals that can exist in the cold polar regions are those with heavy fur.

Many systems have been devised for classifying the world's climates. One of the simplest lists five major types:

Tropical Rainy Climates: Every month is warm, and the total rainfall is heavy.

Dry Climates: Less than 20 inches of precipitation per year. (Precipitation is the total amount of water that falls. It includes not only rain, but also snow. The snow is melted before being measured.)

Warm Rainy Climates: Average temperature of the coldest month is between 27° and 64° F. Annual rainfall is 20 to 40 inches.

Humid Cold Climates: Average temperature of the coldest month is below 27° F. Summers are warm to hot, and yearly precipitation is generally less than about 25 inches.

Polar Climates: Average temperature of the warmest month is less than 50° F. Precipitation is scant.

The following table shows average temperatures and precipitation in selected cities throughout the world.

CLIMATE DATA FROM AROUND THE WORLD					
Location	Average Temperature* Jan.	July†	Precipitation (Inches) Jan.	July	Annual
Arica, Chile	72	61	0	0	0
Asunción, Paraguay	83	63	5	2	52
Berlin, Germany	20	60	1.5	3	23
Chicago, Illinois	25	75	2	3	33
Honolulu, Hawaii	71	79	4	1.5	32
Khartoum, Sudan	74	93	0	2	6
London, England	40	61	2	2	24
Los Angeles, Calif.	56	73	3	0	15
New Orleans, La.	56	83	5	7	64
Peking, China	25	80	0.2	10	24
Rangoon, Burma	76	88	0	23	100
Sydney, Australia	71	54	3	5	45
Vancouver, Canada	37	64	9	1	41
Verkhoyansk, Russia	−58	59	0.1	1	5
Winnipeg, Canada	0	68	1	3	20

*In degrees Fahrenheit

†Khartoum is for May, Rangoon for April—the hottest months in these cities. Arica, Asunción, and Sydney are south of the Equator; in these cities July is a winter month.

Water
NaCl=Salt

What the World Is Made of

EVERYTHING in the world is made from one or more elements. The water we drink, the ground we walk on, the air we breathe, and all other substances are made from elements. There are more than 100 elements that occur on earth. Scientists believe that the same kinds of elements are present on the other planets and on the stars.

Oxygen, copper, and mercury are examples of elements. There is nothing in oxygen but oxygen, nothing in copper but copper, nothing in mercury but mercury. This rule is followed by each of the elements. They are the substances that have not been formed from simpler substances. It is these elements that combine in many ways to make the great variety of things that we find all about us.

Names have been given to all of the elements. Scientists do not always use the whole word when they write the name. They use a shorthand way of writing it. They call this the *symbol* for the element. O is for the symbol for oxygen. H is the symbol for hydrogen.

Some of the elements are more common than others. The table on page 112 shows the most important or best known ones. At room temperature some elements are gases, some are liquids, and some are solids. One column of the table contains the letters G for gas, L for liquid, and S for solid.

By studying the chart carefully you discover that just two of these elements are liquids at normal room temperatures. They are mercury and bromine. Some of the other elements are gases, but most of them are solids. Among the more common gases are argon, chlorine, fluorine, helium, hydrogen, neon, nitrogen, and oxygen.

Most of the solid elements are metals. The metals are elements that are lustrous or shiny. All the metals except mercury are solid at ordinary temperatures.

Almost everyone has heard the word *atom.* An atom is simply the very smallest particle of an element that still is like the element. An atom is so small that it can be seen only under the most powerful type of microscope.

Atoms themselves are composed of still smaller particles called *protons, neutrons,* and *electrons.* The electrons have one kind of electrical charge which is called negative electricity. The protons have a positive electrical charge. The neutron is a mass of material the same weight as the proton. It, however, has no electrical charge. It is electrically neutral.

An atom has most of its weight concentrated in its *nucleus,* or center. The nucleus consists of protons and neutrons. Each proton has 1 unit of weight. Each neutron has 1 unit of weight also. The electrons of an atom have practically no weight. The electrons move about in paths outside the nucleus. Sometimes the atom is described as a tiny solar system. The nucleus at the center is in the position of the sun. Around the nucleus, electrons move in much the same way as planets revolve around the sun.

Electrons and protons attract each other. So, as the negative electrons move around in their orbits, they are always attracted toward the center by the positive protons. The attractive force of the electrons and protons for each other helps hold the atom together. But just as a rock whirled at the end of a string keeps going around, the electrons keep going around the nucleus of the atom without being pulled into it by the protons.

Although single atoms have been photographed through powerful microscopes, the photographs do not show atomic structure as clearly as drawings or models. Scientists were able to explain atomic structure even before it was possible to take photographs of atoms. They learned about this structure by studying how atoms behave.

Every one of the elements has a different number of protons. In the Table of Leading Elements on page 112, the column which gives the *atomic number* tells the number of protons. For each proton in an atom there is an electron. So the atomic number also tells the number of electrons in the atom of an element. Thus the element with atomic number 1 (hydrogen) has 1 proton and 1 electron. The element with atomic number 2 (helium) has 2 protons and 2 electrons, and so on up to atomic number 92 (uranium).

This is not the highest atomic number for an element. There are now more than 100 known elements, and some atomic researchers believe that there are many more to be discovered in the future.

The atoms of different elements have different weights as well as different atomic numbers. The weight assigned an element is called its *atomic weight*. The atomic weight tells the total number of protons and neutrons combined in the nucleus of the atom. The atoms of all elements except hydrogen have neutrons. Since most hydrogen atoms have only 1 proton and no neutrons, hydrogen atoms are the lightest of all. The atomic weight of hydrogen is about 1. Oxygen is about 16 times heavier than hydrogen, so oxygen has the atomic weight 16.

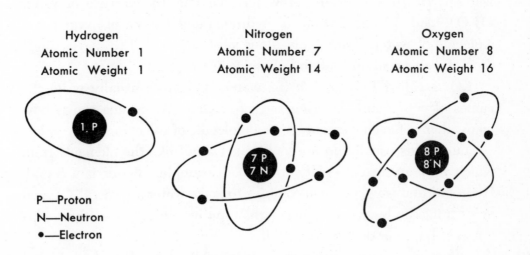

Hydrogen
Atomic Number 1
Atomic Weight 1

Nitrogen
Atomic Number 7
Atomic Weight 14

Oxygen
Atomic Number 8
Atomic Weight 16

P—Proton
N—Neutron
●—Electron

This means that an atom of oxygen has a total of 16 protons and neutrons. It also means that any number of oxygen atoms would be 16 times heavier than an equal number of hydrogen atoms. The atoms of sulphur weigh twice as much as the atoms of oxygen so sulphur has the atomic weight 32. The atomic weights of the elements are in the last column of the table.

The atoms of elements combine in many different ways to make the great variety of things we have around us. Sometimes 2 atoms of the same element cling together to form larger particles. This is true of some of the gases such as hydrogen and oxygen. For example, 1 atom of hydrogen unites with another atom of hydrogen. This results in a *molecule* of hydrogen. The chemist would write it $H + H = H_2$. More often atoms of an element combine with atoms of one or more other elements to form molecules of different kinds of substances called *compounds*.

For example, hydrogen unites with oxygen to form a substance that is entirely different from either one of them. The compound formed is water. Thus hydrogen (an element) + oxygen (an element) = water (a compound) or $2 H_2 + O_2 = 2H_2O$. To a chemist this means that 2 molecules of hydrogen unite with 1 molecule of oxygen to make 2 molecules of water. Water is always formed by these two elements combining in this way. The smallest particle of water that still remains water is called a molecule of water. That is, the particle of water (H_2O), made of just 2 atoms of hydrogen and 1 atom of oxygen, is a molecule of water. Each molecule is very, very small so that a single drop of water contains millions of molecules.

H_2O is called the *formula* for water. Chemists usually write the names of compounds by using such formulas. A formula shows how many atoms of each element are in a molecule of the compound.

Compounds usually do not look or act at all like the elements from which they are made. Water is a good example. Water is a liquid. Hydrogen and oxygen which combine to make water are gases. Oxygen helps things to burn, hydrogen burns rapidly, but water neither helps things to burn nor does it burn itself.

Sodium is a silvery white metal. It is a solid but soft and easily cut. Placed on water it reacts violently with the water and gives off a great

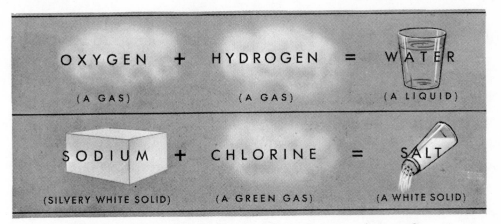

See how these elements combine to make new substances?

deal of heat. Chlorine is a green, poisonous gas. When chlorine and sodium unite to make a compound, what do you suppose is formed? Everyday table salt. This is another good example of a compound that is different from the elements of which it is composed.

The following are some compounds whose common names you know.

Compound (common name)	Elements in the compound	Formula	Chemical name
Table salt	Sodium, Chlorine	$NaCl$	Sodium chloride
Sugar	Carbon, Hydrogen, Oxygen	$C_6H_{12}O_6$	Glucose
Iron rust	Iron, Oxygen	Fe_2O_3	Iron oxide
Baking soda	Sodium, Hydrogen, Carbon, Oxygen	$NaHCO_3$	Sodium bicarbonate
Limestone	Calcium, Carbon, Oxygen	$CaCO_3$	Calcium carbonate
Hydrochloric acid	Hydrogen, Chloride	HCl	Hydrochloric acid
Lye	Sodium, Oxygen, Hydrogen	$NaOH$	Sodium hydroxide

One group of compounds is called *acids*. Acids are sour. The sour taste of lemon juice, grapefruit juice, and vinegar shows that they are acids. One very important acid, called hydrochloric acid, is formed when hydrogen unites with chlorine. It has the formula HCl.

Another group of compounds is called *bases*. Lye is a good example of a base. Its chemical name is sodium hydroxide and its formula is NaOH. Almost all bases have a metal, like sodium, united with oxygen and hydrogen.

When a compound unites with another compound, two or more new compounds may be formed. For example, when hydrochloric acid is added to sodium hydroxide, two new substances, salt and water, are formed. $HCl + NaOH = NaCl + H_2O$. You see, the elements in the original substances have traded partners. The acid is sour and will seriously burn the skin. The base is bitter and will also burn the skin. But when they are combined they form two entirely different substances. This is just one of thousands of chemical changes that go on in the world about us.

One of the most important of chemical processes goes on in plants. They get carbon dioxide from the air through tiny openings in the leaves, and water comes up from the soil through the roots and stems. By the action of sunlight on the wonderful green substance in plants called *chlorophyll*, the plants are able to use the carbon dioxide and water to make the sugars and starches out of which the plants build their tissues. This process is called *photosynthesis*.

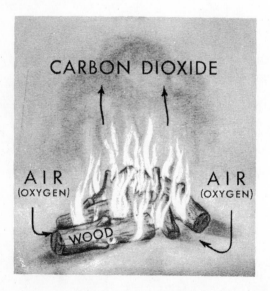

CARBON DIOXIDE

AIR (OXYGEN)

AIR (OXYGEN)

WOOD

When a substance such as coal or wood is burned, the carbon in it unites with oxygen from the air to form carbon dioxide, and the heat given off is the result of this chemical action. The food we take into our bodies is "burned" in much the same way, combining with the oxygen we breathe to give us warmth and energy.

When baking soda is mixed with an acid such as

that in sour milk, a chemical action causes carbon dioxide to be given off. This is why many cooking recipes call for baking soda and sour milk in making cakes or biscuits. The carbon dioxide gas pushes its way up through the cake and causes the cake to rise. An acid is combined with baking soda to form carbon dioxide in one kind of fire extinguisher. Oxygen unites with iron to cause rust. These are all important chemical reactions.

Many of the materials in our world are *mixtures*. Air is one of the most common mixtures. It has several elements and compounds all mixed together. They are oxygen, nitrogen, argon, water vapor, carbon dioxide, and a few other substances. In a mixture the substances are not chemically united with each other. This means they can be present in varying amounts. In air, for example, the amount of oxygen can change. In a compound the amount by weight of each element is always exactly the same. Here is a list of a few mixtures whose names are familiar to you.

Mixture	Principal substances in the mixture
Sea water	Water, salt, magnesium chloride, other minerals
Milk	Water, butterfat, minerals, protein
Wood	Carbon-hydrogen-oxygen compounds
Gasoline	Carbon-hydrogen compounds
Ink	Water, solid dyes

The elements are all of interest and value but some of them are especially interesting, either because they are so common, or because of their great value to man. A few are interesting because of their unusual behavior.

Carbon (C) is an important and necessary element in all living things. It is also the great fuel. It appears in an almost endless number of compounds. Coal is mostly carbon. In the presence of oxygen and under the influence of heat, carbon burns readily.

Oxygen (O) is one of the most common elements, and one of the most useful. It combines readily with nearly every other element, hence besides its abundance in the air, it appears in a great many compounds. It is discussed more fully in the story "The Ocean We Cannot See," beginning on page 139.

Hydrogen (H) is a gas. It is the lightest of all the elements and is the most common substance in the universe. Stars, for example, are mostly hydrogen. Hydrogen is used in the making of many different chemical compounds.

Helium (He) is also a light gas. Unlike hydrogen, it will not burn and so is used for inflating balloons and blimps. Helium occurs in sizeable amounts in certain natural-gas wells in North America, Russia, and South Africa.

Mercury (Hg) is one of the few elements that is a liquid at normal room temperatures. It is a heavy, silver-colored metal that is used in thermometers, electrical switches, and in certain types of bright electric lights known as mercury-vapor lamps.

Iron (Fe) is one of the most abundant metals in the earth's crust. It is necessary for all forms of plant and animal life. Iron is very important as the basic substance in steel and iron alloys, from which thousands of different manufactured products are made.

Sulphur (S) is a yellow, nonmetallic solid element that is found in both the earth's crust and in sea water. Most sulphur is used to make sulphuric acid and other useful chemical compounds. Coal and fuels made from petroleum sometimes contain sulphur that causes air pollution when these substances are burned.

Radium (Ra) is a metallic element, quite rare and of great value. Because of the tiny particles and the energy which radium atoms give off spontaneously, radium is said to be "radioactive."

Uranium (U) is one of the heaviest of all elements. It is a metal, and is radioactive like radium. One of its forms, uranium 235, is used in making nuclear bombs.

The scientists who first split the atom discovered many of the secrets of atomic energy. They knew that in all ordinary chemical reactions, such as the burning of fuel and explosions of gunpowder, only the electrons change their position, or are rearranged in orbits outside of the nucleus. They found that the source of atomic energy is the breaking up of the nucleus within the very center of the atom. The very rapid and continuous splitting of nuclei, called a *chain reaction,* is the basis for some nuclear bombs and for nuclear reactors that are used in electric generating plants.

Iron is used chiefly in the making of steel (below).

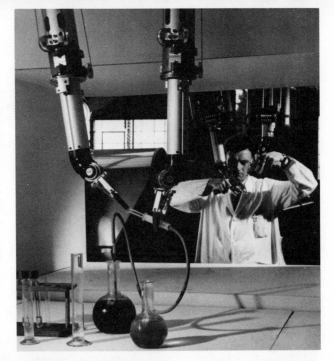

Radium and other highly radioactive materials are handled by remote control (above), because they give off rays that are harmful to living things.

Uranium is the principal fuel used in nuclear power plants such as the one shown above.

Oxygen and hydrogen are often used in welding (near right).

Helium is used to inflate weather balloons (far right).

Many uses have already been found for atomic energy. Atomic fuels are used to run ships and submarines, and to provide power for electric generating plants. People are working, right now, on atom-powered airplanes and rockets. In the future we may have atomic fuels for almost every power use.

Chemists are people who study the way materials in our world are made, and how these materials behave. In the past, chemists spent much of their time discovering what the different substances in the world were composed of.

In our modern world, the job of the chemist has changed somewhat. Chemists are now interested in creating new substances. They try to produce in their workshops substances that do not occur in nature. Through experimentation, they have produced new combinations of

Argonne National Laboratory

This machine
is used to help
scientists study the
tiny particles
in atoms.

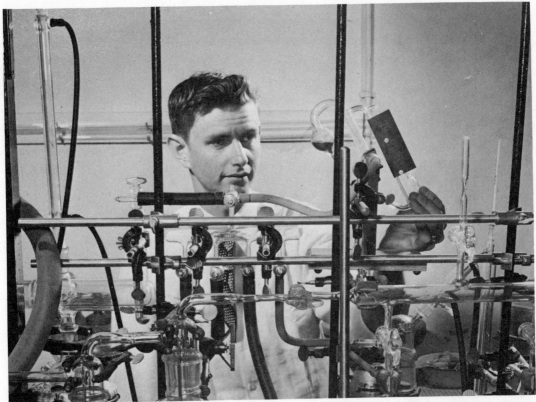

Courtesy Indiana University

Today, many chemists are at work developing substances that will improve our way of life without harming the environment or wasting precious natural resources. For example, cars may someday run on hydrogen (which can be obtained from sea water) or on fuel made from coal (which is far more abundant than petroleum).

elements that do not occur naturally in the world. Such substances are called *synthetics*. Nylon, polyester, plastics, and many kinds of medicines are among the thousands of synthetic materials that man has made.

Plastic is one of the most useful man-made products. It can take almost any form. It can be made into thin flexible sheets, rigid tubes, soft sponges, or solid objects. Anything from raincoats to weather balloons can be made from plastic.

And we can expect new and improved synthetic products in the future. Chemistry will continue to change and improve our way of living. 111

TABLE OF LEADING ELEMENTS

Element	Symbol	Form of Matter	Atomic Number	Atomic Weight*
Aluminum	Al	S	13	27
Antimony	Sb	S	51	122
Argon	Ar	G	18	40
Arsenic	As	S	33	75
Barium	Ba	S	56	137
Bismuth	Bi	S	83	209
Boron	B	S	5	11
Bromine	Br	L	35	80
Cadmium	Cd	S	48	112
Calcium	Ca	S	20	40
Carbon	C	S	6	12
Chlorine	Cl	G	17	35
Chromium	Cr	S	24	52
Cobalt	Co	S	27	59
Copper	Cu	S	29	64
Fluorine	F	G	9	19
Gold	Au	S	79	197
Helium	He	G	2	4
Hydrogen	H	G	1	1
Iodine	I	S	53	127
Iron	Fe	S	26	56
Lead	Pb	S	82	207
Lithium	Li	S	3	7
Magnesium	Mg	S	12	24
Manganese	Mn	S	25	55
Mercury	Hg	L	80	201
Neon	Ne	G	10	20
Nickel	Ni	S	28	59
Nitrogen	N	G	7	14
Oxygen	O	G	8	16
Phosphorus	P	S	15	31
Platinum	Pt	S	78	195
Potassium	K	S	19	39
Radium	Ra	S	88	226
Silicon	Si	S	14	28
Silver	Ag	S	47	108
Sodium	Na	S	11	23
Strontium	Sr	S	38	88
Sulphur	S	S	16	32
Tin	Sn	S	50	119
Tungsten	W	S	74	184
Uranium	U	S	92	238
Zinc	Zn	S	30	65

*Many of the elements have atoms of slightly different weights, and the weights given here are the usual or close to the average for each element. For instance, while most uranium has an atomic weight of 238, it also exists in slightly different forms with weights of 234 and 235.

The Story of Heat

FEW THINGS are so important to us as heat. Heat cooks our food and warms our homes. It does a great deal of work for us, furnishing energy in steam engines to run trains and machines. In fact, a proper amount of heat is necessary to life itself.

People were a long time finding out what heat is. They used to think that it was a mysterious fluid that went in and out of materials. Of course, they could not see it and neither did it seem to have any weight, because an object does not weigh any more when it is hot than it does when it is cold. About 150 years ago, Sir Humphrey Davy proved that ice could be melted simply by rubbing two pieces together, although everything around it was below freezing. Then scientists began to see that heat is not a fluid after all.

We know now that heat is a result of the motion of atoms or molecules, the tiny particles of which every substance is made. These molecules are always moving. In solids they simply vibrate about fixed positions. In liquids the molecules wander about within the entire body of the fluid. They move even more freely in gases, for the molecules of a gas are much farther apart. The speed with which they move depends upon the amount of heat.

As water is heated, its molecules move back and forth faster and faster. When air is heated, its molecules move faster. When the pavement and sidewalks are heated by the sun, their molecules vibrate more violently.

Heated material will cool off when heat is no longer applied to it. This means the motion of its molecules slows down. An object would be the coldest possible if its molecules did not move at all. But scientists tell us that nothing on earth has ever been that cold. Such a point would be reached only at a temperature of about 459° below zero, which is called *absolute zero*.

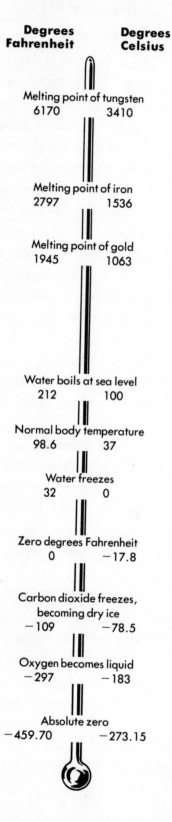

Degrees Fahrenheit | **Degrees Celsius**

Melting point of tungsten
6170   3410

Melting point of iron
2797   1536

Melting point of gold
1945   1063

Water boils at sea level
212   100

Normal body temperature
98.6   37

Water freezes
32   0

Zero degrees Fahrenheit
0   −17.8

Carbon dioxide freezes, becoming dry ice
−109   −78.5

Oxygen becomes liquid
−297   −183

Absolute zero
−459.70   −273.15

Therefore, everything has some heat in it. When we say that a substance is cold, it is not true that it contains no heat. It merely means that it is cold compared to something else, perhaps colder than our bodies, so that it feels cold to our sense of touch.

Practically all substances expand when they are heated. As the increased heat causes the molecules to move more rapidly, they bump against one another more often, crowd each other farther apart, and take up more space. On the other hand, these same substances contract again as they are cooled.

It is this expansion and contraction that enables thermometers to measure the temperature. A common type of thermometer uses a liquid such as mercury or alcohol. The liquid creeps up the tube as the heat causes it to expand. The markings, called degrees (°), are usually on either the Fahrenheit scale or the Celsius scale. (The scales are named for the scientists who invented them.) On the Fahrenheit scale, the freezing point of water is 32° and the boiling point 212°. On the Celsius scale, the freezing point is 0° and the boiling point 100°. Sometimes temperatures are given followed by the letters F or C, to indicate which scale is meant; since Fahrenheit is used most often in the United States, all references to temperature in this book are to Fahrenheit.

The expansion of materials by heat has been made use of in other instruments, such as the thermostat which regulates temperatures in buildings. But while heat does useful work for us, it also gives us many problems. Telephone and telegraph lines that seem tight in the winter sag in the summer. Pavements sometimes buckle up in bumps during hot summer days. Spaces must be left between the ends of railroad rails so that the rails will have room to expand. Dishes, especially thin water glasses, may crack or break when hot water is poured on them suddenly.

Add or take away enough heat and even greater changes take place. Cool a gas sufficiently and it becomes first a liquid and then at a still lower temperature a solid, just as water vapor when cooled changes first to water and finally to ice. On the other hand, almost all solids, when enough heat is applied, melt, then change to gas.

The temperatures at which different substances change from one state to another varies widely. Water, you know, freezes at 32°. Air becomes a liquid at —313.6°. Gold does not melt until it is heated to 1945.4°, but another metal, mercury, is already a liquid at ordinary temperatures and does not become a solid until it is cooled to —38°.

An object may for some reason have the ability to do work. If so, the object possesses energy. Heat is a form of energy. Other forms of energy are light and electricity; another is chemical energy, that energy which is stored up in such things as food and fuel; still another is mechanical energy, like that of falling water. Heat may be changed into some of these other forms and each of these other forms of energy may be changed into heat.

We usually think of getting heat by burning something. The fuel we burn to warm our homes has chemical energy stored in it. Burning releases the chemical energy.

In an electric toaster or electric stove, electrical energy is changed to heat energy. When the sun's rays strike the earth some of the light energy is changed to heat.

Rub two blocks of wood or any solid objects together and then feel their surfaces. They feel warm to you. These are examples of mechanical energy being changed to heat energy. Whenever machines have parts that rub together, heat is produced. The rubbing is called friction. Heat produced in this way where it is not needed means that energy is being wasted, and oil is used in machines to cut down the amount of friction, thus saving energy as well as wear.

When heat is used to make steam to run an engine, we have an example of heat energy being changed to mechanical energy.

Heat can get from one place to another in different ways. In solids heat travels by *conduction*. If several small pieces of paraffin are attached along an iron rod and one end is held near a fire, the pieces of wax will melt and drop off, one after another. The piece of wax nearest the fire will drop off first, then the next one, and so on until

FIRE   PARAFFIN

they all drop off. Finally the end of the rod away from the fire will get hot too.

How does the heat travel along the rod? The fire causes the molecules in one end of the rod to move faster. They in turn bump their neighbor molecules. By this increased bumping and speeding up of

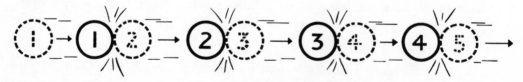

the motion of adjoining molecules, the heat is carried all along the rod. When the molecules at the far end are moving fast enough, that end also is hot.

In this way heat travels through solid materials. Cooking utensils usually have wooden handles because wood does not conduct heat nearly as well as metals. Stone and glass are also very poor conductors; so are all gases and all liquids except mercury.

Heat travels through liquids and gases principally by *convection* rather than by conduction. All the water in a pan placed on a hot stove will soon get warm. First the molecules near the fire absorb heat energy. They move faster and occupy more space thus becoming lighter. This makes them rise to the top of the pan. The cooler, heavier water then moves down in the pan and is warmed. The movement of the water as the warmer water continues to move to the top and the cool water moves down is called a *convection current*.

Hot-water heating systems carry heat from the furnace to the radiators by convection. As the water is heated it rises in the pipes, to be led from the top of the furnace through pipes to metal radiators. From there heat is given out by the hot water to the surrounding air.

Warm-air furnaces make use of convection currents in heated air. The air is warmed in a furnace. It then rises through ducts to the rooms of the house. Cooler air from the rooms returns to the furnace, is heated, and again moves upward. (In modern warm-air furnaces, a motor-driven fan, or blower, helps move the air upward. The blower, inside the furnace, makes the system more efficient and use less fuel.) Winds are mostly huge convection currents caused by the unequal heating of the surface of the earth and the air above.

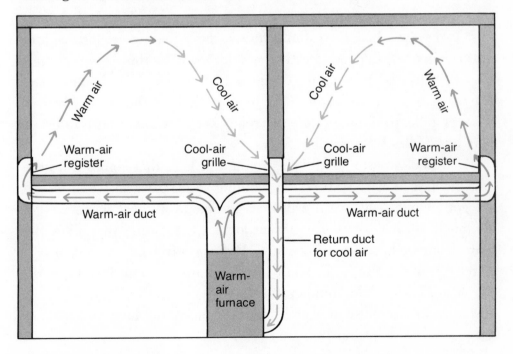

You get the warmth from a bonfire mostly by radiation.

Heat energy travels in another important way known as *radiation*. Our heat from the sun comes to us in this manner. The sun gives off radiant energy. This energy comes through space and when it strikes the earth, some of it changes into heat energy. Radiant energy is not easy to describe, because it is much like light energy except that you cannot see it. Radiant energy escapes from all hot objects. It is given off by a fire. You have felt the heat strike your face when you stood in front of a bonfire or fireplace.

Have you ever noticed how warm it is near the sunny side of a building, even when it is cold away from the building? Radiant energy changes to heat energy when it is absorbed by something.

In the winter we are interested in keeping warm. We do this in at least two ways. Inside we build fires to heat the air around us, and out-of-doors we depend mostly on additional clothes. Our clothes keep us warm by preventing the heat from leaving our bodies. The heavier or warmer our clothes, the more body heat they trap. Instead of keeping the cold out, our clothes really keep the heat that is radiated from our bodies from getting away.

We are not able to control the amount of heat that comes from the sun, but just as we use fuel and clothing to keep warm when we do not get enough heat, we use devices to take away heat when we get too much. In hot weather, we wear loose, light clothes that allow the heat of our bodies to escape easily. We use refrigerators to cool and thereby preserve our food. Many buildings are air conditioned to keep the air at a comfortable temperature.

Man has accomplished a great deal in controlling heat and making it do useful work for him.

Light and How We See

EVERY morning the sun edges its way up in the east and a new day begins. The sun with its abundant energy lights the daytime world. The rays of the sun are so strong that, even on a cloudy day, there is much light.

Light is a form of energy. That means it can do work. For one thing, it enables us to see.

But sunlight does something else which is of the greatest importance to our earth. It enables plants to grow. The leaves absorb some of the sun's energy and use it in making plant food which the plants must have.

Some objects have a kind of light within themselves, like hot coals and electric light bulbs and fireflies and certain little animals that live in sea water. These things which contain their own light are said to be *luminous.*

Most objects we can see only because they reflect light to our eyes. You see this book or the house next door or the tree in the yard because of reflected light. These objects, having no light within them, are *non-luminous.*

Light travels more than 186,000 miles in 1 second—faster than anything else in the whole universe. It takes only about 8 minutes for light to reach us from the sun, 93,000,000 miles away. But even at that rate, it takes many years for light to reach us from the stars.

If you look at Arcturus, one of the closest stars, it will twinkle in your eyes tonight with light that left that star 40 years ago. That is, the light of Arcturus traveling at a speed of 186,000 miles a second, takes 40 years to reach the earth. The distance from the earth to a star usually is measured by the length of time it takes the star's light to reach us. Following this method, we say that Arcturus is 40 light years away. Some of the stars that we see are many hundreds of light years away.

119

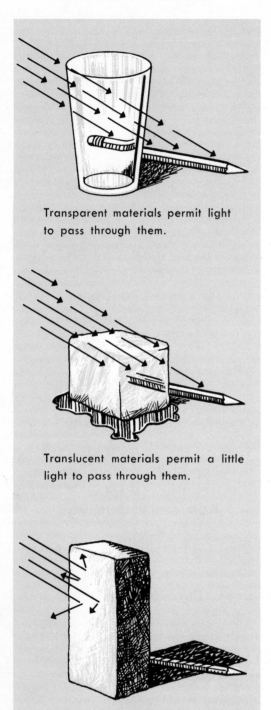

Transparent materials permit light to pass through them.

Translucent materials permit a little light to pass through them.

Opaque materials permit no light to pass through them.

An unusual ceremony took place at the Chicago World's Fair in 1933. Light from Arcturus, flashing on a machine, started a signal which officially opened the Fair. This was of particular interest because the light that arrived from Arcturus in 1933, had left the star forty years before, in 1893, the year that Chicago held its first great fair.

Light travels in straight lines. It cannot curve around buildings or around corners. If it did you would be able to see around objects. You would be able to see objects, many miles away, even around the curved surface of the earth. But because light travels in straight lines, it is possible to see only a few miles in any direction. The distance beyond which we cannot see around the earth is called the *horizon*.

The horizon is not a real line. It marks the point where the earth's curve stops light from reaching your eyes from any object beyond that point. The horizon is always as far as you can see.

Light can pass through some materials such as glass and water and cellophane, and these materials are said to be *transparent*. You can see through transparent materials.

Other materials permit a little light to pass through them, but not enough to see through them clearly. Frosted glass, ice, and waxed paper are examples. These materials are *translucent*. Solid objects which permit no light at all to pass through them are said to be *opaque*. Such objects cast a shadow when light shines upon one side of them.

The shadows we are accustomed to are not completely dark because light gets into them from other directions by *reflection*. If you stand with your back to bright sunlight, you cast a shadow in front of you. If you drop some object like a piece of paper in the middle of your shadow, you will be able to see the paper because there is enough light in the shadow to reflect from the paper to you. That light is reflected from dust and moisture particles in the air, and from buildings and trees and other objects. So, by reflected light you are able to see things that are not in direct sunlight.

The fact that dust and moisture reflect light is of tremendous importance, because that gives us a more even amount of sunlight. At great heights above the earth, where there is neither dust nor moisture, it is quite dark in directions other than toward the sun because there is nothing to reflect and scatter the light.

If a surface is rough, the light that strikes it will be scattered in many directions. Light scattered by such a surface is *diffused*, like the light from frosted bulbs or windows.

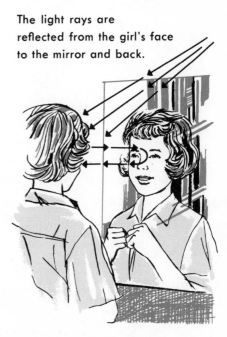

The light rays are reflected from the girl's face to the mirror and back.

A smooth opaque surface reflects light evenly. This is true of a mirror, or of a piece of brightly polished metal.

You see yourself in a mirror because the light is reflected from you to the mirror and back again. We usually use flat mirrors, but there are curved ones. The shiny metal in the back part of an automobile headlight is curved so as to reflect the rays from the light bulb into a small area on the road ahead.

121

Some of the large telescopes which scientists use to study the stars have huge reflecting mirrors to help collect light from a star and direct it to the eye of the observer or to a camera mounted on the telescope. The largest telescope in the world, located in Russia's Caucasus Mountains, has a 236-inch glass reflector which enables scientists to study stars thousands of light years away.

Put a knife in a glass of water and notice how the knife seems to be bent. If you move the knife over to the other side of the glass, it will appear to bend in the other direction. Actually, it is the light reflected from the knife which is bent by the water. This bending of light rays is called *refraction*.

Place a coin in a shallow bowl and back away until you can no longer see the coin over the edge. Then ask another person to pour water in the bowl slowly while you watch. When the water level rises to a certain height, you will suddenly be able to see the coin again. It is not floating, as you know, but the water has bent the light rays and makes the coin appear to be where it is not.

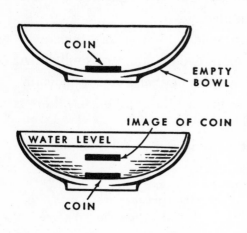

An example of refracted light.

If you see a fish from the edge of a pond, it is not actually where your eyes tell you it is. The fish is below that spot, and the mistake you make is caused by refraction. From where the fish is your head will appear to be some distance up in the air, for refraction will work both ways.

The reflection and refraction of light sometimes plays more serious tricks on people. Desert travelers have often been confused by seeing what looks like an oasis a short distance away only to have it disappear when they approach it. What happens is that certain conditions of the atmosphere cause refraction so that an object seems relatively close when it really is far away below the horizon. Such a vision is called a *mirage*.

There is no lake in the distance. It is a mirage.

This scene shows the land as it actually appears.

White light is really a mixture of several colors of light. Often when bright sunlight passes through an aquarium or glass bowl filled with water, it forms a rainbow on the floor or nearby wall. This has the same pattern of color as a rainbow in the sky caused by the sun shining through a shower of rain. The colors are violet, indigo, blue, green, yellow, orange, and red—always arranged in that order. The rays of sunlight are being bent, and some light bends more than other light. The violet part bends the most, the red the least, and the others are in between.

Objects appear to us the same color as the color of the light they reflect. A red apple reflects red light and absorbs the other colors. A yellow pencil reflects yellow light and absorbs the other colors. A white object reflects all colors of light equally and a black object does not reflect any light. Thus, black is the absence of light.

White cellophane permits all the colors of light to pass through it. Colored cellophane permits only the light of that particular color to pass through. Blue cellophane, for example, permits only the blue part of the white light to pass and blocks out the other colors. The colors that we see are always the colors that come to our eyes from the objects we are looking at.

Pieces of curved glass called *lenses* bend light. Because of this they have many important uses. The most common use is in eye glasses, but lenses are also used in microscopes and telescopes.

There are two kinds of lenses, concave which curve inward, and convex which curve outward. Eye glasses are either concave or convex, depending on the need of the person who wears them. Concave lenses

123

spread the light out over a wider area, and convex lenses gather the light toward a point, called a *focus*. If sunlight is focused through a large convex lens, enough heat can be directed to one spot to start a fire in paper or wood shavings.

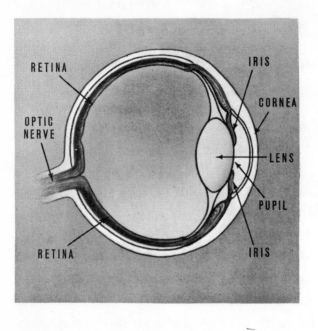

The most wonderful lenses are those in our own eyes. These are not made of glass, of course, but they work the same way, and bend light as a glass lens bends light. Light comes in through the *cornea*, a thin membrane which covers the outside of the eye. Then it passes through a small opening, called the *pupil*. The lens, directly behind the pupil, bends the light so that it strikes the *retina*. The retina is a tiny screen with nerves running to it which carry an impression of what is being seen directly to the brain.

If more light is needed on the retina in order to see well, the pupil opens wider. The size of the pupil is regulated by the *iris*, a membrane surrounding the pupil, which gives eyes their color. The eyeball is filled with a liquid which helps the eye keep its shape and helps the lens to bend the light rays and focus them on the retina.

When we look at distant objects, the lenses of our eyes become thinner. When we look at close objects, the lenses get thicker. The change is regulated by small muscles that work without our thinking about them. Sometimes, however, the lenses do not change shape easily or the shape of the eyeball is such that images do not form properly on the retina. The lenses need help. It is then that people wear glasses. The glasses help direct the light so that it forms clear images on the retina.

Magic that Flows Through Wires

PRETEND that your family has just purchased a farm or new country home. It is equipped with all of the conveniences of modern living—except that there is no electricity! Imagine what fun it would be to watch your house being wired for electricity for the first time. First, workmen would sink a huge pole into the ground and attach long wires to it. This is called the power line. Then connecting wires are run from the line to the house.

Inside you would see strange things happening—holes being bored in walls and floors, and wires enclosed in wrappings being run all through the house. The ends of the wires in every room are fastened to the sockets into which electric cords are plugged.

Now the electricity can be turned on. Someone pushes a switch in the living room and the room is suddenly bright with light!

Something certainly came into the house through the wires. But how? What was it? We know about some of the many kinds of useful work electricity can do for us, but it is a little harder to understand just what electricity *is*. Of course, it is a form of energy. It may be changed into other forms of energy like heat and light and mechanical energy, and these other forms may in turn be changed into electrical energy.

Scientists think that an electric current is a flow of electrons through a conductor. Electrons, you remember from the story "What the World Is Made Of" beginning on page 101, are the tiny particles of matter found in the atoms of all elements. The electrons move about in a particular atom, and some of them can easily be made to move about in a piece of material, in which case the material is called a conductor. The conductor may be a copper wire, or a strip of zinc metal, or perhaps a liquid.

There are two common ways of producing an electric current: chemically in batteries, and mechanically by generators.

First let us see how batteries work. The electric current that lights a common flashlight bulb comes from a battery called a dry cell. The cell is not really dry. There is a wet paste in it. The dry cell is a store of chemical energy. When the chemicals act on each other, they free electrons which flow through a conductor, thereby producing an electric current. Most dry cells are made with a carbon stick surrounded by a paste of chemicals, including ammonium chloride, and placed inside a zinc metal container which, in turn, is enclosed in cardboard.

No electric current is produced unless the electrons are given a chance to move through a conductor from the zinc metal and back to the carbon stick. The chemical action of the paste on the carbon stick and the zinc container causes electrons to move away from the carbon and to the zinc.

You will remember that electrons are tiny particles having negative charges of electricity. The place where they collect, which in this case is the zinc metal, is called the *negative electrode*. After they flow through the conductor and return to the battery, they come to the *positive electrode*, which in the dry cell is the carbon stick. These electrodes are often marked — and +. Keep in mind that the negative electrode (−) gives off electrons and the positive electrode (+) gets them back, that is, the electrons flow from the negative toward the positive.

The path provided by the conductor between the electrodes is called a *circuit*. The object of a switch is to *close* the circuit, permitting the current to flow when it is wanted; and to *open,* or break, the circuit by causing a gap in the conductor when the current is not needed. Dry cells are very convenient for supplying small amounts of electricity, such as that used to light a flashlight, to operate toys, and to do many other small jobs.

Let us see how two dry cells would be wired to an electric bell to ring it. A wire runs from the negative electrode of the first battery to the positive electrode of the second one. From the positive electrode of the first battery a wire goes to a switch (in the form of a pushbutton). From the other side of the switch the wire goes to one binding post of the bell. From the other post of the bell a wire runs back to the negative electrode of the second battery. When the circuit is closed by pushing the button, electrons flow through the circuit and, as explained on page 136, cause the bell to ring.

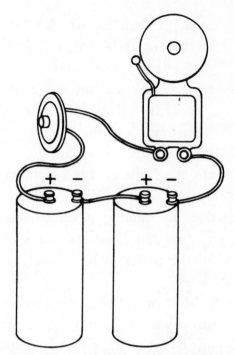

Storage batteries such as those used in automobiles are wet batteries. They are made of cells having a liquid in them which acts on metals to free the electrons, just as the ammonium chloride paste does in the dry cell.

The liquid is a solution of sulphuric acid. It acts chemically on two sets of metal plates. One set is made of lead, the other of lead peroxide. When the circuit is closed, electrons are freed at the lead plate, making it negative. These electrons then flow out through the circuit and do their work as they move back to the positive plate of the battery.

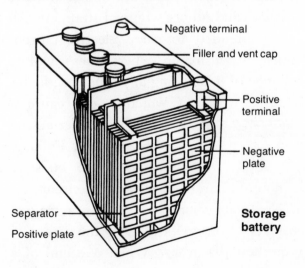

Negative terminal

Filler and vent cap

Positive terminal

Negative plate

Separator

Positive plate

Storage battery

In an automobile the electrical energy from the storage battery does several different jobs. It operates the starter, the lights, and various accessories.

It supplies a spark in the spark plugs to explode the gasoline which causes the engine to run. Such batteries are used to do these larger tasks because they furnish more current than dry cells do. But there is a more important way in which these two types of batteries are different.

In a dry cell the source of the energy exists in the chemicals, and when they lose their energy, the battery is worn out. While a wet storage battery must first be "charged" with energy before it will operate at all, the energy can be replaced as it is used. Thus, by keeping it charged, it will go on storing and releasing energy. The charging is done by running an electric current into the battery from a generator. The charging process stores up chemical energy in the solution and on the plates to be released as electrical energy when the circuit is closed.

Most of the electricity we use in our homes and in industry comes directly from electric generators. If we followed the electric wires from our house to their very beginning, we would arrive at a power plant. In the power plant we would find huge generators being turned by engines or by water power.

There was a time just over a hundred years ago when we did not know how to produce electric current by means of generators. Then one day an Englishman by the name of Michael Faraday discovered he could cause electrons to move through a wire without using chemicals.

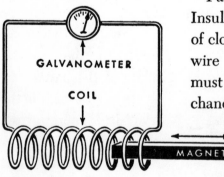

Faraday made a coil from *insulated* wire. Insulated wire is wire with material made of cloth and rubber wrapped around it. All wire intended to carry electric current must be insulated where there ·is any chance of it touching any other conductor which would cause a "short" or sidetracking of the current. Faraday fastened the ends of wire together as shown in the picture. This made a complete circuit. He then produced a current of electricity simply by moving a magnet through the coil. He had caused electrons to move along the wire.

Faraday made another important discovery. When one end of a

This huge electric generator is a producer of great power.

magnet was thrust into the coil, the electrons moved in one direction. When the magnet was pulled out, the electrons moved in the other direction. This back and forth motion of the electrons is called *alternating current*.

Other scientists quickly made use of Faraday's discovery to produce huge generators by which large amounts of electric current could be made. But no matter how big they are, or how complicated they look, modern generators all work in much the same way as Michael Faraday's little combination of wire coil and magnet.

To turn a generator requires power. In many communities, the power plants are run by engines which burn fuel, but where water power is available, it is much cheaper to let the falling weight of the water do the work. Thus our largest and cheapest sources of electric power are at dams and waterfalls. Huge hydroelectric plants such as those at Grand Coulee Dam on the Columbia River, Hoover Dam on the Colorado River, and Niagara Falls, each furnishes enough power to supply factories, cities, and farms over wide areas around them.

Water from above the dam or falls runs off into huge tubes called penstocks which lead to turbines below. A turbine is a large spiral fan-like blade that turns when the water runs onto it. The turbine then turns a generator.

In most large generators, huge magnets on a shaft revolve within the coil of wire, or *armature*, which remains stationary and is connected to the power line directly. However, in many generators the magnetic field is stationary and the armature revolves. Then to make a circuit with the power line, brushes are attached to the ends of the coil to make contact with a conductor as the armature turns, or revolves.

So we find that electricity can be produced in amounts that are very large or very small; that there are large currents and small currents. Let us see how an electric current is measured.

The rate of flow is measured in *amperes*. The more electrons moving along a wire, the greater the number of amperes.

Everything takes some push to move it. This is true of electrons. The push or force that does this is measured in *volts*. The more volts, the more push. A battery of 12 volts, for example, will push more amperes of current through a certain closed circuit than a 6-volt battery will in the same length of time.

Some conductors let electricity pass through them easily. Copper wire is one of the best and most commonly used conductors. Electricity passes through other materials only with great difficulty. Such substances have a high resistance. The amount of resistance of a conductor is measured in *ohms*. A wire 10 feet long has twice as much resistance as a piece of the same wire 5 feet long. The greater the resistance, the more volts are required to carry the same number of amperes. Scientists have determined exact standards for measuring these quantities and a volt of electricity is the amount of push required to put one ampere of current through a resistance of one ohm.

The electric wires in most homes in the United States carry about 120 volts. The average automobile battery produces 12 volts, which is developed by 6 cells of 2 volts each. Of course, these voltages are small compared with the many thousands of volts developed by each generator found in a huge electric plant.

Watt is another term used in measuring electricity. It refers to the amount of work done every second by a current of one ampere under a pressure of one volt. Most light bulbs are marked in watts. A 60-watt bulb burning for 1 hour uses 60 watt-hours of electric energy. However, since a watt is a very small unit, a *kilowatt* (1,000 watts) is generally used in speaking of larger quantities of electric power. The electric meter in your home measures the amount of electric energy you use in *kilowatt-hours*.

We have come to depend a great deal upon electricity in our everyday living. Perhaps first of all comes electric lights. The resistance of the filaments in the light bulbs as the electrons pass through them causes the filaments to glow and produce light. This glowing is called *incandescence*. Thomas Edison invented the incandescent light after searching for years to find a satisfactory material for the filament. He also invented or improved many other electrical devices.

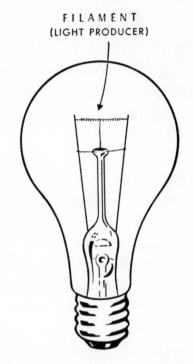

FILAMENT
(LIGHT PRODUCER)

In electric irons, toasters, and stoves, the electrons cause the wire through which they pass to become very hot. These devices use much more electricity than do ordinary electric lights.

The electric motor is an important part of many household appliances. It runs the washing machine, the vacuum sweeper, the electric fan, the electric refrigerator, and dozens of other machines. It also runs the dentist's drill. In industry electric motors have a wide variety of uses.

A motor is the opposite of a generator. Instead of producing electricity, the motor uses it to make the armature revolve and do work. The motor changes electrical energy into mechanical energy.

But important as electricity is in our daily lives in producing heat, light, and power, these are by no means all of its valuable uses. It is used in putting a thin coat of one metal such as silver or copper over another metal, which is called electroplating. Some kinds of silverware are made of brass with a silver coating. The bumpers and door handles on your car are probably chromium plated.

Electricity is used in producing the X-ray and is valuable to the physician in many other ways. It carries messages for us over telegraph wires, and enables us to talk over the telephone. It makes possible the broadcasting and receiving of radio and television programs. In fact, it would take several pages just to list the more common uses of electricity.

Magnetism

LONG AGO a kind of black iron ore that was quite unusual was discovered in the earth's surface. It would attract iron objects to it. When a long, slender piece of the ore was hung by a string, it always came to rest in a north-south position. The stone was used to guide travelers and so was named leading-stone or lodestone.

Magnets were known to the Chinese very early in the history of civilization, and the compass was in use in Europe before the 15th Century. Columbus used a compass on his voyage across the Atlantic in 1492. Today we are not dependent on pieces of lodestone—our magnets are man-made. They are doing many important tasks.

A small magnet may be purchased for a few cents and many children have them for play-things. Such magnets are made of a bar of iron or steel. Some are horseshoe or U-shaped. If one end of the magnet is touched to small objects made of iron such as tacks or small nails, the magnet will pick them up. Other substances like copper, gold, paper, rubber, or wood will not be affected by it. Iron, cobalt, and nickel are the only substances that are highly magnetic.

There are some substances, mainly antimony and bismuth, which are weakly repelled or pushed away by a magnet.

Every magnet has two poles. One end is called a north pole and the other a south pole. Sometimes the poles of magnets are marked N and S. Both poles will attract iron. Yet they are different, as a simple experiment will show.

Tie a string around the center of a bar magnet so that the magnet will hang level. Then let the magnet swing freely. Hold the N pole of a second bar magnet near the N pole of the first magnet. You will see the N pole of the suspended magnet pushed away by the N pole of the other magnet. Now hold the S pole of the second magnet near the S pole of the first. They, too, repel each other. Hold the S pole near the N pole. These poles are attracted to each other. So you see there

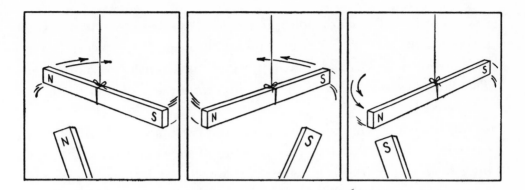

is something different about the N and S poles of magnets. The north and south poles attract each other, although the north repels the north, and the south repels the south. This is always true of all magnets.

The space around a magnet in which a piece of iron is affected by it is called the *magnetic field*. Even though the mysterious force cannot be seen, it is possible to get a picture of the magnetic field. If a piece of glass or paper is placed over a magnet and iron filings are sprinkled upon it, the filings will arrange themselves in curved lines that seem to come out of the north pole and pass in a curve around to the south pole. These lines are called *lines of force*.

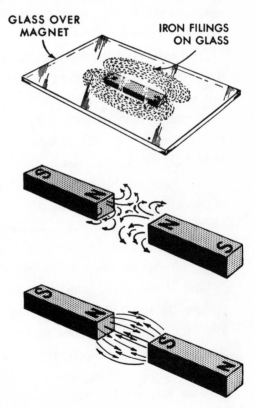

GLASS OVER MAGNET

IRON FILINGS ON GLASS

If two north poles or two south poles are placed near each other, their lines of force seem to push against each other and crowd apart. This suggests why like poles repel each other. If a N pole is placed near a S pole, the lines of force run from the N pole directly to the S pole. The arrangement of the iron filings suggest that the lines of force are pulling the opposite poles together.

Every piece of magnetized iron

133

has a north and a south pole. If this iron is cut in two pieces each piece is a magnet with a north and south pole. These pieces in turn may be cut in halves and they, too, would have north and south poles. This fact gives us a clue to the condition of a piece of iron when it is magnetized.

You remember that all materials in the earth are made up of small particles called molecules. Iron is made of molecules. Probably each little molecule of iron is a magnet. When the molecules of a piece of iron are mixed, with their poles pointing in every possible direction, then the iron is not magnetized. But when the molecules get lined up so that many of their south poles point in one direction and the north poles in the other, then the iron is magnetized.

There are several ways to magnetize a piece of unmagnetized iron. Each method arranges the tiny molecules so that their N and S poles point in opposite directions. Here is an easy way to magnetize an ordinary nail. Hold it in one hand with the point out. Then stroke the nail with the N pole of a magnet. Stroke toward the point of the nail and stroke it several times. Then the nail itself will be a magnet and it will attract other pieces of iron.

Iron will keep its magnetism for quite a long time, but will lose it more quickly than a piece of hard steel. For this reason, most bar and horseshoe magnets are made from steel. Because such magnets keep their magnetism so long, they are often referred to as permanent magnets. Magnets of soft iron which can be magnetized easily but which lose their magnetism easily are called temporary magnets.

The most useful kind of temporary magnet is the *electromagnet*. It is made by passing an electric current through a covered wire that has been coiled around a soft iron bar. The strength of an electromagnet can be increased by wrapping more turns of wire around the iron, or by increasing the amount of current passing through the coiled wire.

One of the most important advantages of the electromagnet is that it has its magnetism only while the electric current is turned on. Electromagnets are a necessary part of many electrical devices. They are the heart of telegraph sounders, electric doorbells, and the huge electromagnet lifting cranes that are used to load and unload scrap iron or heavy iron bars.

You cannot pick up a piece of wood, a glass or paper dolls with a magnet.

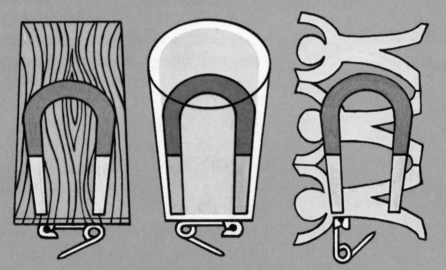

You can pick up a metal pin through the piece of wood, the glass, and the paper because the metal pin is in the magnet's "magnetic field."

This will work with any material that isn't too thick—even your finger. Try it and see.

The magnet pulls the clapper arm.

The clapper strikes the bell and breaks the current.

The clapper arm springs back.

The flow of electricity again pulls the arm back.

Let us see how an ordinary electric bell operates. When the button is pushed to close the circuit, electricity flows through the coils of wire in the electromagnet. The magnet pulls the arm to which the clapper is attached, making the clapper strike the bell. As it does so, the path of the electric current is broken so that the magnet loses its strength, and the spring in the arm causes the arm to snap back. But when it snaps back, the path of the electric current is closed again and the magnet, regaining its force, pulls the clapper arm toward it once more, again causing it to strike the bell. Of course, this action takes place very rapidly, giving the bell almost a steady ring. It will continue as long as the button is pushed.

Magnets are a necessary part of every electric motor and electric generator. They are used in telephone receivers, in loudspeakers, and in many other devices. A doctor will use a small bar magnet to remove particles of iron or steel dust from the eye. In a tape recorder, a magnet transfers electrical signals representing sound to a tape coated with a substance that is easily magnetized. A similar system is used by large computers, with the electrical signals representing numbers.

The earth itself is a huge magnet. Most of this magnetism is probably caused by electric currents deep inside the earth's core. Like any other magnet, the earth has two magnetic poles. One of these poles is in northern Canada near the North Pole.

The other magnetic pole is in Antarctica near the South Pole. A magnetic field exists around the earth just as it does around an ordinary iron magnet. (See drawing at right.)

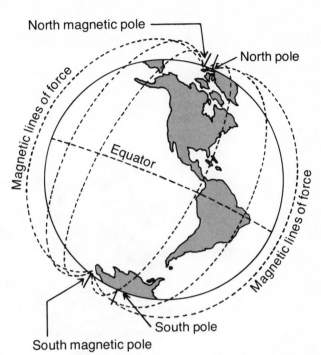

A compass needle is a small magnet balanced so that it will turn freely. The N pole on the compass points toward the magnetic pole in the north. Since the northern magnetic pole is not exactly at the North Pole the compass needle in most parts of the earth does not point true north. The compass is a useful direction finder, however, even though it is not perfectly accurate. A compass should not be used near large iron objects, as they will influence the compass needle and may make it point in the wrong direction. In using the compass you must permit the needle to come to rest. Then you turn the base of the compass until the letter N on the face of the compass is at the pointer of the needle. The other letters on the compass then correctly indicate South, East, and West.

A skydiver's parachute catches air in its canopy as it floats to the ground.
Although air is invisible, we know it is there and this picture shows one reason
why—it offers resistance to any object moving through it, in this case enough
to slow the parachute's descent to a safe speed.

Photo by Gerald Keefe

The Ocean We Cannot See

W E LIVE on the bottom of a tremendous ocean, an ocean so big that it covers the whole world, yet we cannot see it. It is not made of water, like the Atlantic and the Pacific and the other oceans; it is made of gas, the gas we call air.

Air is everywhere on the surface of earth, and it is wrapped around the earth like a blanket many miles thick. There is air in your yard, in your room, and even inside you, because you are breathing it in and out all the time. It is the most common thing in the world, yet one of the most valuable. Neither animals nor plants could live without it.

We cannot see air, but we can feel it. Wave your hand rapidly past your face. Note how you can feel the air passing your fingers and also how you can feel it on your face. You can feel it every time the wind blows because wind is nothing more than air in motion.

Have you ever watched a leaf floating to the ground? It falls slowly because it is so light in relation to its surface area that the air under it holds it back. If there were no air, a leaf and a rock would both fall at the same speed. The next time you are outside, open your coat and hold it wide. Then try to run. The reason that you cannot run as fast as usual is because your coat catches so much air.

The same idea saves the lives of people who jump from airplanes. The big, billowing parachutes, donned for jumping, catch the air and thus keep the parachuters from falling too fast to make a safe landing. On the other hand, in order to lessen the resistance of the air and thereby increase their speeds, airplanes and automobiles have streamlined shapes.

A light wind enables a kite to fly because the push of the air is then strong enough to hold up the kite. An airplane flies because its propellers or jet engines force the plane ahead through the air rapidly. The air pushes more strongly against the lower surface of the moving wings than it does against the upper surface, creating a lifting effect that holds the airplane up. Yes, air is a very real substance even though we cannot see it.

Air is a mixture of several gases, but most of it is oxygen and nitrogen. Oxygen is the part used in breathing and in burning. One of the ways that nitrogen helps us is in diluting the oxygen, as pure oxygen is too strong for most purposes. Air is about 21 per cent oxygen, 78 per cent nitrogen, and only one per cent other gases, chiefly argon, carbon dioxide, and water vapor.

We breathe out carbon dioxide from our lungs. Carbon dioxide is formed whenever something is burned. Therefore the air in cities, where many people live close together, does not have quite the same composition as air in the country. With all the breathing and all the fires in a city, you may wonder why the air does not become more and more filled with carbon dioxide. The reason this does not occur is because the leaves of plants take it in, remove the carbon for their use and give most of the oxygen back into the air.

The farther above the earth we go, the thinner the air gets. There is much less air on a high mountain than there is at the seashore. People carry tanks of oxygen with them to help them breathe when they fly higher than about 3 miles. There is a very small amount of air at a height of 100 miles or even higher but almost all of the air is below 15 miles, and half of it is below 3½ miles.

Probably you have noticed that bubbles come to the top of a pan of water when it is being heated. Tiny bubbles also collect on the side of a glass of water that is left in the warm sunlight. So there is air in water too.

Once some children thought that they would make the water for their goldfish pure by boiling it. So they boiled the water and then cooled it. The goldfish died very soon after they were placed in it. Heating the water had driven out almost all of the air. Of course, if the water had been left to stand again for a few days, it would have absorbed some more air. Running water or water that is being churned around takes up all the air that it can hold quite rapidly. Plants growing in the water help put oxygen into the water.

There is also air mixed in the soil. Worms and other animals that live in the soil need air to breathe. You can see air bubbles come to the top when you pour water into a jar of dirt. The water forces the air out from between the particles of dirt.

When you blow into a rubber balloon you crowd air into it and make it stretch. You are pushing the tiny little particles, or molecules, of air against one another and, of course, they push back. If you blow too hard and the push becomes too great, the rubber breaks. The force of compressed air is made to do many kinds of useful work. It holds up our automobile tires. It operates air brakes on trains and trucks, and it runs rock drills and many other machines.

Like most other substances, air expands when heated. Warm air is lighter than cool air, so warm air rises. The air near the ceiling of a room is usually warmer than that along the floor. In the story about wind, we learned that winds are caused mostly by the heavier, cool air rushing in as the lighter, warm air rises.

Fire needs oxygen. Nothing can burn without it. Firemen keep oxygen from reaching a fire by pouring water on it. They also use chemicals to put out fires. These prevent enough oxygen from getting to the fire by forming a gas that smothers the flames. Casting dirt on a small out-of-doors fire will quickly smother it.

If ever your clothing should

Modern fire-fighting equipment helps these firemen do their job. The
firemen climbing the ladder are using the hook and ladder truck.
Look at the other trucks, and see if you can tell what their uses are.

catch on fire, cover yourself up quickly with a rug or blanket. Even
a coat, if used in time, might be large enough to cover the flames
and snuff them out. Above all, do not run, as that only fans the
flames. If you have nothing to cover yourself with, drop down quickly
in a heap, and try to smother the flames under you. It is hoped, of
course, that none of our readers takes such dangerous chances as to
play with matches or fire, which every year cause many children to be
seriously burned.

If a small lighted candle is placed on a table and a glass or fruit
jar turned upside down over the candle, the flame will flicker for
a moment and then go out. It burns until it has used up most of the
useful part of the air, that is, the oxygen, and then it cannot burn
any longer. Any form of animal life put in a closed chamber will die
too, as soon as a good part of the oxygen is breathed up.

142

You may have noticed someone blowing on a small fire or fanning it to make it burn faster. The wind created in this way supplies the fire with more oxygen. Of course, the oxygen does not burn. If it did, a lighted match would start flames all around you. But it enables other things to burn.

Some things burn easily. Some burn very little or not at all. Paper and wood burn easily because the carbon in them combines easily with the air. Iron does not burn at ordinary temperatures. It does, however, combine slowly with oxygen, a process called rusting. When nails or other pieces of iron are moist they combine with oxygen more easily and rust more quickly. Unpainted tools and machines made of iron soon rust when they are left outdoors. Paint prevents rusting by keeping the oxygen away from the iron.

The oxygen we breathe into our lungs combines with the food we eat in a kind of slow burning process. This process keeps us warm and provides us with energy. After great exertion we often find ourselves breathing quickly and hard. It is a sign that we are in need of more oxygen.

Air has weight. This you readily can discover by weighing a spare tire when it is soft, and then weighing it after it has been inflated with air. At sea level, a cubic foot of free air, air that has not been compressed, weighs about one and one-fourth ounces. The air inside a room that is a little larger than a two-car garage weighs about 100 pounds.

2,000 pounds of air

This weight of air piled up for mile after mile presses down upon the surface of the earth with tremendous force. Of course, the higher you go, the less the weight of the air above. At sea level this pressure is 14.7 pounds on each square inch.

It is pushing on this open book, right now, with a force of almost 2,000 pounds, or one ton.

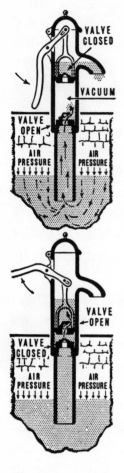

Why is it then, that you can hold the book so easily if there is such an enormous weight pressing down upon it? Because the pressure of the air is equal in every direction. The same pressure is pushing up from under the book and between the pages and in all directions around the book, so that you have only the weight of the book to hold.

We make use of air pressure in many ways. You drink a soda or some other liquid through a straw by using air pressure. As you suck the air out of the straw, the pressure of the air outside pushes the liquid up into the straw and from there into your mouth.

Have you ever pumped water from a well? If so, the chances are you used a *suction* pump. When you pushed on the handle of the pump you lifted some water out of the pipe. At the same time air pressure caused more water to rise in the pipe for you to pump out on the next stroke. The pressure of the air is strong enough so that it can push water up into a pipe to a height of about 30 feet, when the air is pumped out of the pipe.

Another use of air pressure is found in the vacuum cleaner. The motor operates a fan which pushes out air, and as it does so more air comes in through the opening at the bottom, picking up the dirt.

The pressure of the air varies from time to time even at the same altitude, depending on the weather conditions. The barometer which measures these changes helps "weathermen" forecast the weather. This is described on page 80 in the story, "How the Weather Affects Us All."

Sounds We Hear

WHEN you sit quietly and listen, you are likely to hear sounds so familiar that you do not notice them. You may hear the song of a bird or the ticking of a clock. But whether you notice them or not, nearly always there are sounds of some kind reaching your ears.

Perhaps you have wondered how these sounds occur. Every sound is made by something vibrating, that is, by moving very quickly back and forth. When a door slams we hear it because the bumping of the door against the casing causes vibrations in the wood. A piano gives off sound when its strings are made to vibrate. You hear your friend's voice because vibrations are set up in his vocal cords as he speaks. Leaves rustle because they are set to vibrating by the wind. All sounds are made by something vibrating.

But how do the sounds reach our ears? They come to us as sound waves. Whenever an object starts vibrating it causes the air nearest to it to vibrate. This in turn sets the air next to it in motion. In this manner the vibrations are passed on until they reach the air nearest our ears. Where this happens the vibrations are heard as sounds.

Vibrations go out just as the circular waves of water expand in all directions when you throw a rock into a pool. If you were to cast two rocks into the pool at the same time the waves circling out from one rock might overlap those spreading out from the second rock, but each series of circular waves would continue, even though they might get mixed up. In the same way several sets of sound waves often cross one another.

The outer parts of our ears help to collect the sound waves and direct them to the eardrum. From there the vibrations are passed

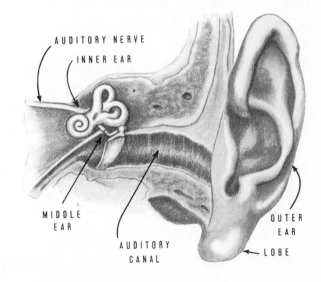

AUDITORY NERVE

INNER EAR

MIDDLE EAR

AUDITORY CANAL

OUTER EAR

LOBE

145

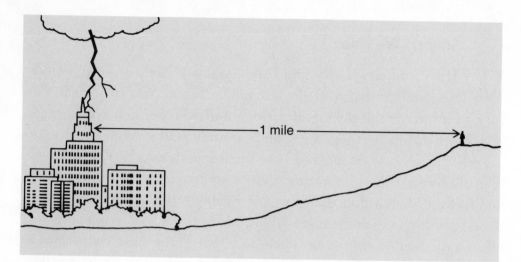

Sound travels much slower than light. The observer on the hill, one mile from the tallest building, does not hear the sound of thunder until five seconds after seeing the lightning flash. This is because sound travels through air at only about 1,100 feet per second, but the speed of light is about 186,000 *miles* per second.

on to other delicate inner parts and finally to nerves which lead to the brain. When the message gets to the brain, the sound is heard.

Sound travels through all materials—liquids, solids, and gases. Have a companion tap the end of the table lightly with a pencil. Then place your ear at the opposite end of the table, and ask your friend to repeat the table tapping. Note how much clearer the sound seems when the ear was placed against the wood. Some day when swimming hold your ears under the water while a companion knocks two stones together in the water several feet away from you. You will hear the sound very distinctly.

Sound travels through some substances better than others. It will not travel in a vacuum (an empty space from which the air has been removed). If an electric doorbell is placed inside a sealed jar and the air pumped out, the sound will get fainter as the air inside gets thinner, although the bell can be seen to vibrate just as strongly as ever. This shows that sound waves must have some material to travel through.

Sound waves move as the molecules of air, or other substance through which the waves travel, bump one another. This requires the expenditure of energy. The stronger the vibration, the louder the sound. But the farther the sound waves travel, the weaker they become.

The bumping continues only so long as there is energy left. When the energy is all used up, the vibrating stops and the sound dies out.

Sound waves travel in air at the rate of about 1,100 feet each second. This equals about 750 miles per hour, or one mile in 5 seconds. A mile in 5 seconds may seem like pretty fast traveling, but it is very slow compared with the tremendous speed of light.

You can see this demonstrated clearly during a thunderstorm. Try counting the number of seconds from the time you see a flash of lightning until you hear the thunder. Divide this number by 5 and you will have the distance in miles to the point where the lightning struck. This simple way of measuring the distance is possible because light is seen almost instantly and it requires 5 seconds for each mile the sound has to travel.

On a warm day sound waves travel a little faster than on a cold day. For each degree the temperature rises, the speed of sound increases about 1.1 feet per second. At 32° sound travels in air about 1,090 feet per second and at 68° it travels about 1,130 feet per second.

When sound waves strike a solid surface, such as a cliff or steep hillside, some distance away, we often hear them a second time as they are reflected back to us. We call such a second sound an *echo*.

Bats make use of echoes to keep from running into obstacles when they fly in the dark. They let out shrieks which their keen ears detect, although their cries are pitched too high for human ears to hear.

When a person shouts into a deep well or even into a barrel, a great jumble of sounds results. This is called *reverberation*. Reflection of the sound occurs over and over again as the sound waves bounce back and forth from one wall to another. Echoes and reverberation some-

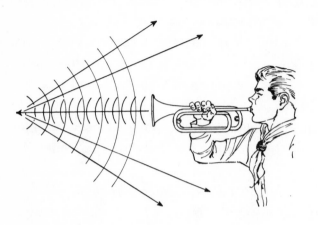

times occur in large rooms and auditoriums unless the buildings are planned properly to avoid such annoyances.

Reflection of sound can be prevented. Ceilings of school corridors and classrooms are often covered with some sound absorbing mate-rial to reduce the reflection of sound. Carpeted floors, window drap-eries, and clothing also help prevent reflection of sound.

When someone drops a tin can on the floor or slams a door, we call the sound noise. When someone draws a bow across the strings of a violin or strikes the keys of a piano, we think of music. What is the difference between noise and music? It is in their different kinds of vibrations.

Scientists sometimes draw pictures to represent sound waves, even though sound waves themselves cannot be seen. The pure sound given off by a flute, for example, might be shown as a regularly vibrating smooth line. This kind of wave represents a musical sound. But the picture showing a noise is very irregular. It has no smooth curves. It is a very uneven looking line. A noise is a sound that gives off irregular sound waves. A musical tone results when a vibrating body gives off regular and uniform sound waves.

MUSICAL SOUND WAVE

NOISE SOUND WAVE

The notes played from the right side of the piano keyboard have a higher tone than those played from the left. This highness or lowness of a musical sound is called its pitch. What makes this difference in pitch? As you know, every sound is produced by something vibrating. The faster something vibrates the higher will be the pitch of its sound.

The middle C on a piano vibrates about 256 times each second. The next C note above (called high C) vibrates 512 times a second. The C note below middle C (low C) vibrates 128 times a second. The

LOW C 128   MIDDLE C 256   HIGH C 512

highest notes on a piano vibrate about 4,200 times a second, the lowest about 28 times.

The human ear is very sensitive. Yet most people cannot hear sounds having fewer than 16 vibrations per second nor more than about 16,000 per second. There are many vibrations in the air which the human ear cannot hear.

The pitch of a note on a stringed instrument depends on the length of the string. The shorter the string, the faster it will vibrate. The pitch of a sound from a horn like a trumpet or a trombone is raised by shortening the length of the vibrating column of air. In an organ, the long pipes produce low notes, the short ones high notes.

Musical sounds also have *quality*. Although the same note or pitch may be played on the piano and violin with the same degree of loudness, the two instruments do not sound the same. The voices of different people do not sound alike. Different vibrating bodies produce different qualities of sound.

Musical sounds, then, besides having degrees of loudness, have pitch and quality. By combining these features of musical sounds in various ways, musicians produce music. A great orchestra has many instruments of different quality playing sometimes in the same, sometimes in different pitches, sometimes softly, and sometimes loudly, to get the musical effects desired.

Commerce & Industry

The Story of Shelter

THERE IS no record old enough to tell us who built the first shelter. Undoubtedly thousands of times in thousands of different places early prehistoric men felt the need of escaping from the heat of the sun or the drive of the storm. They huddled under trees or in thickets or used whatever was at hand to protect themselves.

Some shelters were fashioned by sticking branches into the ground and lacing other branches in and out among them. Other shelters were made from skins tied to sticks set into the ground.

Of course such shelters were only crude screens or windbreaks. But even today, a few primitive tribes still live in such windbreaks. A picture on the next page shows the type of windbreak once used by people of Tierra del Fuego.

Probably the first home that man lived in was a cave. Certainly it was a natural abode for one who spent most of his day prowling about in search of food. Because such shelters were not to be found everywhere, in some parts of the world early men dug and carved out rooms in the sides of cliffs. They usually made the entrances several feet above the ground, using ladders, often made of woven vines, to get in and out of their dwellings. Those ladders were pulled up when not in use, in order that the cliff dwellers might secure safety from possible enemies.

As long as man depended entirely upon hunting for his living he could well use caves and dugouts. But after he had learned to tame animals and accumulate them in flocks and herds, he was forced to live wherever he could find grazing lands for them. He used skins for a cover as he stretched out on the ground to rest. Later he sewed skins together and hung them over a pole to make a tent. In time he learned to set a pole at each corner of a square with a taller one in the center, and spread overhead a covering for a roof. Such a tent, really one of the first forms of a house, could be taken down quickly and set up again at the next stopping place.

Tents made from the skins of their flocks were the only dwelling places Abraham and Isaac and Jacob knew. And the Bedouin Arab today still pitches his tent wherever he decides to stop on the desert, and rolls it up again whenever he is ready to move.

About ten or twelve thousand years ago man learned to sow the seeds of grasses in the fertile river valleys and to harvest them in due season. As a farmer he found it best to settle down in one place. For the first time man was faced with the need of a fixed abode in which he and his family could dwell and store his possessions. His

American Museum of Natural History

152   Indians of South America's Tierra del Fuego region once used simple windbreaks for their shelter, as shown in this model.

Farmhouse, Japan

Village Home, Malaysia

Riverside Home, Peru

Photos: Japan Air Lines; United Press International (Malaysia); Ghana Information Office; Organization of American States

Village Homes, Ghana

fumbling efforts to build a home were the beginning of the many kinds of buildings which we have today.

There is little in the world that has not undergone growth and change. So too, man and his ways of living have a long story of development behind them. Houses did not suddenly come to be. Their builders, like inventors, began where others had left off. Using this knowledge of what had begun before, they gradually invented new forms and made improvements in the old.

The first building must have been an enclosed space with a roof, because there is no way to build a room except with walls, and no way to keep out the weather except with a roof. A few long branches set in the ground, perhaps in a circle, with the tops bound together, would provide the framework. A hole could be left at the top out of which smoke might rise from a fire. Then the framework could be thatched by weaving grasses in and out among the branches, leaving an opening at one side for an entrance.

The African Zulu builds his thatched dome-shaped hut today in such a manner. So do many other modern primitives. An excellent way of learning how prehistoric people built their shelters is to study the homes of modern primitives in different parts of the world. They are built much as their ancestors built them thousands of years ago.

As wood was used in the forested regions, clay and mud had to be used in the places where there were few trees. Among the earliest places where man settled was the valley of the Tigris and Euphrates rivers. In ancient times that region was called Babylonia. There on the treeless plains man, in need of building material, noted the way in which the heat of the sun baked the soft mud into something like stone. So he began to shape chunks of mud into bricks and dry them in the sun. Before long he had learned to stiffen the bricks by mixing straw with the clay.

Clay has been used, too, for centuries, in the construction of wattle and daub dwellings. The walls of such shelters are made from the branches of trees interwoven with twigs, reeds, and grass called wattle, and daubed, or plastered, with clay. Many of the thatched wattle and daub cottages which may be seen in various parts of Europe today have been plastered both inside and out with clay.

This is a wattle and daub dwelling.

Wherever stone was abundant, man has made use of that in the construction of his buildings. Among the ancient builders to leave great structures of stone were the Egyptians. They were the builders of the Pyramids, each pyramid being the tomb of a king, or pharaoh, as the ruler of Egypt was called. By that time man was no longer an awkward groping worker. He had become a skilled craftsman.

Thus it was that through the ages man learned to build not only great buildings but great cities and empires. One after another, Babylonia, Egypt, Greece, and Rome rose to great heights. As they fell back, their works were largely demolished, but still the knowledge and skill of building lived on.

The Europeans who first discovered and explored America found the Indians living in primitive shelters. Their dwellings were constructed of the materials at hand, and varied according to the skills and the needs of their owners. The tribes that roved the Great Plains in search of herds of buffalo erected light skin tents called

155

tepees. Other tribes living in the wooded regions of the country depended upon bark to cover the framework of their wigwams. Those who were farmers built more permanent dwellings such as the long houses of the Iroquois and the pueblos of the Hopi.

The first American colonists built small log cabins with tamped earth for floors and greased paper for window panes. But as soon as possible they began to construct houses more like those they had known in their native countries. Many of them were skilled craftsmen. And so it was that America came to have Spanish houses in Florida and Louisiana, Dutch houses in New York, and various types of English homes in most of the thirteen colonies along the Atlantic Coast. It was Thomas Jefferson who introduced the Greek and Roman style of building in America with his home, Monticello.

Colonial styles of architecture often are used today in designing houses. However, many other influences such as the Swiss, German, Russian, and Scandinavian are to be found in the styles of buildings in various sections of the United States. All styles have marched westward with the settlement of the country.

Man was content with one, two, and three story buildings until the beginning of the Machine Age when great numbers of people began living in the cities. Apartment buildings were erected to accommodate the greater number of families who wanted to live close to their work. The skyscraper, also, became a familiar building in business and industrial centers. Such tall buildings were possible because of the availability of steel for structural purposes.

Today man is not dependent upon the region where he lives for material to build his house. Transportation makes almost any material available. Neither is he dependent upon his own efforts to construct his shelter. He can call upon architect, contractor, electrician, interior decorator, painter, and many others to help him plan, build and furnish his home.

Every building tells its own story. It speaks of wood and stone, of marble and brick; it speaks of style and workmanship, of builder and purpose. But more than that, it speaks of the people who live within. Much of the history of any community could be written from the story of its buildings.

This famous painting of a farm scene is called *The Gleaners*.

The Story of Food

SOMEWHERE in man's early history, he learned that the best way of securing a good supply of food was by sowing the seeds of plants and cultivating the soil. That discovery changed his whole manner of living. Instead of roving the countryside in search of food for himself and his flocks and herds, he was able to settle down in one place. He then discarded his tent for a permanent shelter. He acquired neighbors, built towns and temples, and found time to develop ways for making life more pleasant. It was the first farmers who really took the first steps toward civilization.

Ever since, man has relied upon cultivating the soil for most of his food requirements. Not only does this yield cereals, fruits, and vegetables for himself, but it produces plant foods for the animals upon which he depends for most of his meat supply.

First in the list of plant foods are the grains from which most of our cereal foods are obtained. Barley, corn, oats, rice, rye and wheat are the leading cereals. Wheat is probably the oldest and most

157

important. It has had a place in man's diet for thousands of years.

The two greatest wheat growing regions in the ancient world were those where our civilization started, Mesopotamia and Egypt. From those countries the raising of wheat spread to Greece and Rome, then northward to other parts of Europe and eastward to Asia. Not until European colonists brought wheat seeds with them was there any wheat raised in the Western Hemisphere.

The wheat which is grown today is not like that grown in ancient times. In those days it was a delicate plant, easily ruined by frost, drought, and disease. As its cultivation spread over the earth the wheat plant adapted itself to different climates and various soils.

About one hundred years ago, Mendel, an Austrian monk, began some scientific experiments with peas. He wrote an account of what he learned. No one paid any attention to it at first, but thirty-five years later scientists began some experiments to carry on the work started by the Austrian monk. Since then, his discovery, now called the *Mendelian Law*, has been used to produce more and better wheat, as well as other food plants. Due to Mendel's work and that of scientists who have followed him, wheat flourishes today in countries where it never could grow before.

Without farm machinery the present tremendous production of food would not be possible. Until the early part of the nineteenth century, most of the work was done by hand. Even after the first metal plow was invented, the farmers were slow to use it. It took them time, too, to see the advantages of Cyrus McCormick's reaper. But once they accepted farm machines they began demanding more and better ones. Today on large modern farms motor-driven gangplows and other attachments prepare the soil; power drills plant many rows of seed at one time; and at harvest time huge combines cut, thresh, and clean the grain in one operation.

One improvement often calls for another. As soon as the farmers were able to grow more wheat they needed better ways to get it to market. Railroad building was hastened, and great storage elevators were built. Cities like Buffalo, Chicago, and Minneapolis became central places for the collection of wheat and the making of flour.

All this has taken place in order that man may have bread. No food ever has surpassed it in general use. Because it appears daily, in one form or another at almost every meal on the tables of the great masses of people of the world, outside of the rice eating regions of Asia, it is often called the "staff of life."

No one knows who first learned how to bake bread. Perchance one day a primitive man while pounding wheat seeds into flour was forced to leave his task. Before his return rain had fallen on the flour and the sun had baked it into a cake. Being hungry, the man tasted it, found it good, and decided to do some baking, using his own crude methods. Undoubtedly the first oven was merely a rock laid in a fire to make the wheat cakes dry faster.

The Greeks were the first people to have public bakeries. The Greek bakers taught the Romans. Gradually the knowledge of bread-making spread throughout Europe. However, the masses of Europeans

International Harvester Company

The first public test of McCormick's reaper was held in Virginia, July, 1831.

did not have wheat flour. They used rye, oats, and barley. This often was combined with ground-up roots and acorns, making a very dark kind of bread.

White flour such as that which we have today was unknown because there were no mills capable of making it. However the Egyptians and later the Romans, by a process of sifting or bolting, managed to produce a flour that was fairly white. The church influenced the production of white flour because the clergy wanted white bread for religious ceremonies. Once the nobility had tasted the white bread they wanted it on their tables. Thus it was that the eating of white bread was associated with wealth and position.

It was only after the invention of modern milling machinery that white bread became a commonplace food. Of all the breads that are made, white bread still remains the favorite. However, in milling white flour, the light golden skin of the wheat seed, called bran, is removed. This removal means a loss of some of the valuable parts of the grain, substances which are important in the growth and health of man and other animals. Chemists speak of these losses as vitamin and mineral losses. Modern millers and bakers often add some of the vitamins and minerals to their white flour or bread mixture. This process is called enrichment.

Through centuries of breadmaking, many countries have developed their own special kinds of breads. Among them are English muffins, Mexican tortillas, Russian dark sour rye bread, German zweiback, Danish pumpernickel, and Scotch oat cakes. Some forms of bread that are particularly American are baking powder biscuits and corn bread.

Not all the wheat is used to make flour for breadmaking. Breakfast cereals take a great share of the wheat grain because much of the corn is used to feed cattle and other animals.

Corn, called maize by the Indians, was an entirely new kind of grain to the first European settlers in America. Those early colonists considered it inferior to the old world cereals. But in their struggle to survive in the new land they learned to like it. Many times it was corn that saved them from starving. Today corn is raised in many countries, but most of it is used to feed livestock.

At first man planted only the seeds of plants native to the region in which he lived. Gradually he became aware of the value of plants growing in other communities. As time went on, many plants were spread from region to region and even from one continent to another.

Originally rice was grown only in China and other parts of the Orient, where it long has been the main food of many people. In the Middle Ages it was brought to Spain by the Moors. Still later it was taken to America by European colonists. Now large quantities of rice are raised in several of the southern states.

Many of our common vegetables originally came from the Old World. Among

United Date Growers Association

Because only the male date flower has an odor inviting to bees, it is vital to collect its pollen, and pollinate each female flower by hand.

them are the artichoke, asparagus, bean, cabbage, carrot, cucumber, cauliflower, celery, egg plant, lettuce, parsnip, pea, okra, oyster plant, spinach, soybean, and turnip. Others like the white and sweet potato, tomato, squash, pumpkin, pepper, and lima bean are native to America.

Fruit probably was one of man's first foods. At certain times it was fairly easy to obtain as he traveled from place to place. Although early man had no idea of spreading the growth of the fruit he ate, he did so when he devoured the pulp and tossed aside the seeds.

Our most common fruits such as the apple, the peach, the pear, the plum, and the cherry, were eaten by people living in the Old World centuries before America was discovered. The early colonists planted the seeds of those fruits rather than the ones of the wild varieties they found growing here, because centuries of cultivation had made

161

The dates are picked individually from permanent platforms.

the Old World fruits larger and sweeter. From those first seeds, hundreds of American varieties have been produced.

The natives of the desert areas of North Africa have depended largely upon the date for food. For centuries this fruit has been exported to Europe and America. Now excellent American dates are grown in irrigated desert valleys such as the Coachella and Imperial Valleys of Southern California.

Man demands meat with his grains, vegetables, and fruits. Great herds of cattle, droves of sheep and swine, and flocks of chickens, ducks, geese, and turkeys are raised each year to fulfill that demand. Along with the beef, lamb, pork, chicken, and turkey, man consumes quantities of cod, salmon, tuna, and other kinds of fish.

At first people had few ways of preserving food for future use. They salted and dried certain kinds of fish and smoked or spiced various types of meat. Later they learned how to can foods, and still later how to keep them fresh by refrigeration long enough to reach distant markets.

J. C. Allen, Century Photos, Inc.

Great herds of cattle are raised to meet man's demands for meat.

Then came Clarence Birdseye of Gloucester, Massachusetts, who had watched the Eskimos freeze fish and meat. He applied quick-freezing to fruits and vegetables. Now due to this wonderful method of preserving food it is possible to have many kinds of fish, meats, vegetables, and fruits the year around in practically as good condition as when they were fresh.

Man lives chiefly on the products of agriculture. When crops fail he faces hunger and sometimes starvation. Many men since Mendel have devoted their lives to the study of soil and plant breeding in order to produce better varieties of plants. Among them were Luther Burbank who performed wonders with certain vegetables, fruits, and flowers, and George Washington Carver who found hundreds of ways to use the peanut and the sweet potato.

Problems of food supply have sometimes caused wars and influenced world events. It was the need for spices that led to the search for a new route to India, and eventually to the discovery of America.

The Story of Clothing

NO ONE knows whether the first clothes were worn as ornaments, or as protection to the body. Quite likely some of the early men tossed the skins of wild beasts over their shoulders to show their skill in hunting. But there hardly can be any doubt that in the cold regions of the earth they used some of the shaggy pelts of the animals they killed to protect themselves from the weather.

One of the tools used in the Stone Age was a sharp-edged scraper. It was used to remove the flesh from the skins of animals. After the scraping was finished the skins were rubbed with fat, then hung over a fire and smoked. This made them dry, strong, and pliable enough to be shaped into the form desired.

The American Indians prepared leather from deerskin in much the same way. From it they made moccasins and other articles of clothing.

The Eskimos have been making garments of fur for a very long time. The skill of an Eskimo woman in making a fur suit, using animal sinews for thread, is remarkable. At the time the white man found them, the Indians and Eskimos had progressed a long way beyond the primitives who merely wrapped themselves up in skins to keep warm.

Some of the early traders who came to America from Europe came for the wealth of the fur-bearing animals here. Nowadays in many civilized countries fur often is used to make entire garments or for trimming.

Leather, which is simply the hides of animals properly prepared by a process known as tanning, is still an important clothing material. While it is used chiefly for making shoes, there are other important uses such as for belts, gloves, and certain types of jackets. The ancient Egyptians were among the first to make fine leather.

The first clothing of those living in warm climates probably consisted of grasses and leaves, or pieces from the bark of trees. Even to this day clothing varies from place to place. Still it does not always hold true that little clothing is worn in the hot climates of the earth, and warm clothing in the cold areas. The natives of cold, windswept

Tierra del Fuego wore little or nothing, while people of desert regions traditionally have worn long, heavy robes.

We do not know when or where man got the idea of making cloth. At the dawn of history he knew how to spin and weave wool, flax, cotton, and silk. For centuries he made fabrics from these four fibers, without finding a suitable fifth one.

At first cloth was worn as it came from the loom. The strip of goods was folded or wrapped around the body in various ways. Sometimes it was draped about the shoulders, sometimes around the waist. Thorns, fishbones, or narrow strips of fabric were used to hold the garment in place. Sometimes the upper part of the fabric was knotted or pinned over one or both shoulders.

Even to this day in some countries, such as India, women dress themselves completely, and often beautifully, too, in one long piece of cloth. First the length of cloth is folded in a manner to form a skirt, and then it is wound about the shoulders. Frequently one end of the cloth is

Pan American Airways

Guatemalan Indians weave beautiful cloth on their hand-made looms.

thrown over the head to make a sort of hood.

Many of the early weavers, like the Peruvians, cut a hole in the middle of a long strip of cloth to make a garment called the poncho. After the owner had slipped his head through the hole he tied the single piece dress into place with a belt. Sometimes the sides of the poncho were sewn together under the arms to form a shirt. The poncho still is worn in some parts of South America.

In temperate climates where the weather is likely to be hot one day and cold or rainy the next, or where it gets hot in the middle of the day and cold at night, people need extra garments which can be easily

discarded. Many an American Indian wore only a breech cloth when the weather was warm and only drew a blanket or robe around him when the weather turned extremely cold.

The first records of the use of definite costumes were found in the tombs of the ancient Egyptians. Many types of dress have been developed since those early Egyptian garments. Some of them were extremely simple in style as, the two important garments of the Greeks, the tunic and the mantle. Others, like the gowns worn by Queen Elizabeth of England, were

Traditional clothing of India

The Peruvian poncho   American frontier   French—early nineteenth century

very elaborate. Some were easy to wear, and others most uncomfortable.

Fashions are determined by many things. Often it is the surroundings in which people live that determine their choice of clothes. There is not a single garment in the entire outfit of a cowboy that is not useful to him in his life on the plains. Other styles may be designed to indicate the rank of the wearer or just to suit some person's whims. It is said that long, hanging sleeves became the fashion in Anne Boleyn's time because she wished to hide a deformed little finger. The fad for wearing starched and pleated ruffs during the reign of Queen Elizabeth started with a Spanish princess who wished to conceal a goiter.

Although climate and environment have played important parts in dress, most of the changes in clothing have come through improvements in the manufacture and use of woven fabrics, or textiles.

Cotton was first used for making cloth in India. Early traders found a ready market for this cloth among the people living near the Mediterranean Sea. At that time the Egyptians and their neighbors were familiar only with linen and wool. Whenever they spoke of the

China—
nineteenth century

Ancient Egyptian   Greek peplos and himation   English—sixteenth century   167

Dan Van Dale Studio

This is Samuel Slater's old textile mill in Pawtucket, Rhode Island.

cotton cloth those early traders called it vegetable wool.

Centuries later the colonists of Virginia began to grow cotton. But its use was small, due to the fact that the fiber clung tightly to the seeds. Separation of the two had to be done by hand. Eli Whitney put an end to the slow and tedious work of cleaning the cotton when he invented the cotton gin in 1793.

About this same time Samuel Slater set up the first American textile mill in Pawtucket, Rhode Island. With the coming of machinery many changes took place. More goods could be produced at a much lower cost. Prices of cloth came down. No longer was it necessary to do spinning and weaving in the home.

Still all the sewing had to be done by hand. The first person to try to make a sewing machine was an Englishman named Thomas Saint. But it was not until Elias Howe, an American, patented a new and better machine that sewing machines came into general use.

Cotton has played an important part in the development of the United States. Large quantities of it are produced in India, China, Egypt, Mexico, Brazil, and Peru. Ever since the first textile machines were invented in England, that country has imported a large part of the world's supply of cotton, and manufactured it into cloth.

Cotton can be produced in greater quantities and at less cost than any other textile. In all the warm regions, and during the hot seasons elsewhere, it is better than wool for most articles of clothing. Some of the fabrics made from it are broadcloth, calico, canvas, cheese-cloth, corduroy, gingham, khaki, lawn, muslin, organdie, percale, poplin, seersucker, voile, and velveteen.

Most of the wool we use comes from the soft fleecy hair that grows on the bodies of sheep. Wool was one of the first materials to be spun and woven into cloth. When early man saw the value of this material, he began to tame and raise sheep. For many purposes, even today, no other cloth is so satisfactory. Wool is especially important for garments used for warmth.

Sheep are raised in many countries, but the greatest amount of the world's supply comes from Australia and the United States. The cashmere goat of India, the angora goat of Asia Minor, and the llama and alpaca of South America yield types of wool that are used for special purposes.

Linen cloth is woven from the fibers of the flax plant. It may have been the first woven fabric ever to be used. Linen garments that were made thousands of years ago have been found in ancient Egyptian temples. For many centuries linen was considered the finest plant fabric. Although cotton eventually replaced flax as the cheapest and most abundant source of cloth, linen still remains the best and most durable fabric for many uses. Ireland long has been the center of the linen industry. Irish linen is world famous. Much of our best linen comes from Ireland.

Century Photos, Inc.

This man is using electric shears to shear sheep.

Nylon is one of the most widely used synthetic fibers. Above left, chemicals are heated in round containers to form molten nylon. Above right, molten nylon is forced through tiny holes in a device something like a shower head, forming filaments that will later be twisted together to make yarn. Below, nylon yarn, wound on bobbins, is inspected before being packaged.

170

Photos courtesy E.I. du Pont de Nemours & Co.

According to legend, a Chinese princess was the first person to notice the work of the silkworm and to devise a way of turning the fine fibers of its cocoon into beautiful cloth. The discovery was kept from the rest of the world for hundreds of years. Then India and Japan learned the secret. The silk industry is still important in parts of Asia today, but in America and Europe silk has been replaced largely by synthetic fibers such as rayon, nylon, polyester, and acrylic.

The first of the synthetics, developed in the 1800's, was rayon, originally known as "artificial silk." It is made from cellulose that is derived from wood or from cotton linters (the fuzz removed from cotton seeds). Rayon has long been used for clothing fabrics and for automobile tire cord.

Nylon is one of the most popular and widely used of all the synthetic fibers. It is made from chemicals extracted chiefly from petroleum. Nylon appeared commercially in 1939, when it was used for women's stockings. Since then, many other uses have been found for nylon, including carpeting, upholstery, and many kinds of clothing fabrics.

Not long after World War II, a number of new synthetic fibers appeared on the market. The most popular of these included polyester, acrylic, and modacrylic. Fabrics made from these fibers are commonly used to make clothing that is wrinkle-free, comfortable to wear, and easy to keep clean. Other synthetics, such as olefin and saran, are used in upholstery, carpets, and—in blends with other fibers—for clothing. In many items of apparel, a synthetic such as polyester is blended with cotton, rayon, or wool to produce fabrics with particular qualities of comfort or durability.

An expressway interchange

The Story of Transportation

SELDOM is there a day when something is not brought to our homes. It may be a letter from Grandmother, a package from the department store, or the daily newspaper. And almost every day, nearly everybody rides somewhere for at least a short distance.

This is made possible by automobiles, trucks, buses, trains, huge oceangoing vessels, and airliners, which carry goods and people quickly and easily from one place to another. All these forms of transportation, which have become as much a part of our everyday lives as clothes and food, have come about in the last one hundred seventy-five years.

From the very beginning, thousands of years ago, people found it necessary to move from place to place. If there was not enough food in one place, they wandered to another, taking along everything they could carry. After learning to till the soil, people began to live in permanent homes, which at first were caves or tree houses or houses built on stilts in a shallow lake.

After that, they carried or dragged home food and other supplies, which often must have required hours of great effort. So they tamed animals like the ox, the llama, the elephant, the reindeer, and the horse and trained them to carry loads.

Then some one discovered that it was easier to roll a burden than to carry it. That discovery led to the development of the wheel, one of the most important things man ever invented. Without it, there could be no automobiles, steamships, trains, airplanes, watches, or hundreds of other things of which the wheel is a part.

No one ever will know what the first wheel was like. But it probably was no more than a thick slice of wood cut from the end of a log. Pegged with a similar one to a sort of axle which was fastened to the bottom of a platform or box, man had his first cart. To be sure, it was crude and awkward, but the cart did carry man and his goods faster, easier, and for greater distances.

Traveling by cart made roads necessary. Roads brought more people together. Exchange of goods and ideas brought new occupations and further improvements in man's living as well as in his transportation. Men became traders, merchants, blacksmiths, innkeepers, and inventors. Wagons, chariots, and stagecoaches were developed.

Long before the wheel, man had found that floating logs tied together into a raft would carry a load on water. By using poles or rough oars, the raft could be moved along the shores of a lake, or over calm stretches of a river.

Then some one using fire and simple tools, hollowed out a log. Although the oldest in existence, this type of boat, known as the

Ava Hamilton

People in many parts of the world still use the ox cart for land travel.

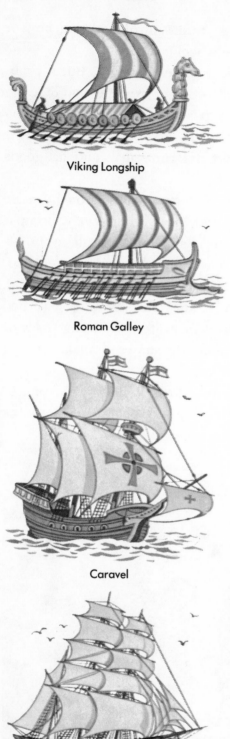

Viking Longship

Roman Galley

Caravel

Clipper

dugout, is used today in some parts of the world.

Later, in many places, primitive men learned to build boats made of light frames of wood or willow reeds. To cover them they used the best materials at hand—birchbark, skins, or asphalt. There were several different types, as for example, the Indian canoe, the Eskimo kayak, and the Welsh coracle.

As man improved in his boat building, the paddle followed the use of the pole. Later came the sail. But these developments did not take place at the same time in all parts of the world. Small Egyptian boats were sailing up and down the Nile when the Phoenicians were building boats rowed by tiers of galley slaves.

With the invention of the compass, ocean navigation became more exact, but it was left for Christopher Columbus to show that the new instrument could be used to guide ships across the ocean. In the mad scramble for the possession of America, European rulers demanded speedier ships. Better design and construction developed rapidly. One type followed another, galleon, frigate, and packet. Then came the clipper, the fastest sailing ship that ever has ridden the waves. Seen in all the world's ports the clipper was queen of the seas until the arrival of the steam engine.

James Watt was not the first person to experiment with steam as a source of power. But he was the first man to successfully put steam to work. His steam engine, invented in 1769, was largely responsible for starting our Machine Age. Its use and continual improvements lifted man from a slow to a fast-moving world.

In 1807 Robert Fulton steamed up the Hudson River in his boat, the Clermont. The steamship Savannah crossed the Atlantic in 1819. To be on the safe side, the ship was propelled by both sails and steam. In 1831 the Royal William made the first complete crossing of the Atlantic entirely under steam power. Within a few more years the famous Cunard Line was offering regular steamship service across the Atlantic.

One day in 1769 there appeared on the streets of Paris a queer three-wheeled carriage which had a copper kettle to move it instead of a horse. At least that is the way it appeared to the people who watched it puff along for a quarter of a mile at a speed of about three miles an hour. The watchers never had seen steam locked up and so they had no idea of its power. They laughed at the horseless carriage which really was a small steam engine. But it was that invention by Cugnot at which the Parisians scoffed and said would never amount to any-

International News Photos

This "horseless carriage," made in 1889, was propelled by a steam engine.

An early locomotive, the *Tom Thumb*, was once defeated in a race with a horse.

thing that was the beginning of all power-driven transportation.

Years later, in 1825, in England, the first steam railroad began service with George Stephenson's famous locomotive, the Rocket, hauling carriages containing passengers and freight. The first regular rail line in the United States ran from Baltimore to Endicott's Mills, a distance of 13 miles. The locomotive used on that first run in 1830 was the Tom Thumb made by Peter Cooper.

In 1869, less than 40 years later, two railroad companies joined their tracks, near Ogden, Utah, to form the first transcontinental rail line in the United States. With that, the settlement of the West was speeded up, and the nation was brought closer together.

As soon as man found a way to harness one source of power, he began to experiment with others. In 1885–6 Gottlieb Daimler, a German, produced the first internal combustion engine, an invention which changed chemical energy into mechanical energy by a series of controlled explosions. In the United States, Charles Duryea is credited with producing the first gasoline-driven horseless carriage in 1893. Soon Henry Ford and others began making automobiles and a new industry was under way.

The invention of the Diesel engine in 1900, and the construction of the first Diesel locomotive in 1925, opened a new era of speed and efficiency in railway transportation. These powerful engines, which are mechanically similar to the gasoline engine, have almost completely replaced steam-powered locomotives on the world's railways. Diesel engines also provide power for trucks, buses, construction equipment, ships, and boats. They are also used, to some extent, to power automobiles.

The first street railways in the world operated in New York City. The first streetcars were horse-drawn vehicles on rails. Meanwhile a few men had been experimenting with the idea of using electricity as a motive power. But it was not until the electric generator, then called a dynamo, was perfected that serious attention was given to the development of the electric railway.

For ages man had watched the flight of birds and wished that he, too, might soar through the air. The famous artist, Leonardo da Vinci, actually made a pair of wings which were fashioned to move up and down by pedals worked by the feet. Although this and other efforts ended in failure, man continued to keep his eyes on the sky. His next efforts in flying took the form of balloons. In 1783, in France, there soared aloft a beautifully painted balloon, made of coarse cloth and

Santa Fe Railway

Freight trains, such as this one, are vital to commerce and industry.

covered with paper. Its owners, the Montgolfier brothers, had sent it up by filling the balloon with hot air and smoke. It came down as soon as the air in the bag cooled. Later the first hydrogen-filled balloon was sent up. Some men actually crossed the English channel in such a balloon. Other flights followed.

Next came the glider, a winged structure which used air currents to stay up and to travel. Samuel Langley put together a glider with a motor which flew across the Potomac River in 1896. Later he launched a similar plane, capable of carrying a man, but it was damaged during the take-off and the flight did not succeed.

This airplane was flown by Orville Wright on the Wright brothers' famous first flight.

Wilbur and Orville Wright began the age of heavier-than-air plane transportation. In 1903 they got their motor-driven plane into the air at Kitty Hawk, North Carolina. They made several short flights, the longest one for 59 seconds and a distance of 852 feet, and landed safely. By 1908 they had sold a model of their latest plane to the United States Government and, also, were showing the machine in

Europe. World interest was aroused. In 1910 Louis Blériot, a Frenchman, flew the English Channel, and shortly afterward Glenn Martin flew from New York to Albany.

In World War I airplanes were at first used only to spot enemy positions and to help artillerymen correct their aim. As planes became sturdier, they were able to carry weapons. They were then used to bomb enemy strongholds and cities, to attack enemy troops, and, increasingly, to fight other planes. Ace fighter pilots became national heroes in their countries. They included Germany's Baron Manfred von Richthofen (called "the Red Baron" because of the color of his plane), William Bishop of Canada, and Eddie Rickenbacker of the United States.

After the war, public interest was greatly increased by such pioneering flights as those of Lieutenant Commander A. C. Read of the United States Navy, who flew from Newfoundland to Portugal by way of the Azores in 1919; J. W. Alcock and A. W. Brown, who made the first nonstop transatlantic flight the same year; Richard Byrd, who flew over the North Pole in 1926; and Charles Lindbergh, who in 1927 made the first nonstop solo crossing of the Atlantic.

Pan American Airways

Travel by jet is comfortable, pleasant, and swift.

Mail and passengers were being carried by plane between London and Paris in 1919. In the United States, the first air mail service was begun in 1918. Within two years a trancontinental mail route was put into operation. Passenger service grew slowly, but by 1930, airlines were spreading rapidly throughout the United States and many other countries. Regular commercial passenger flights were being flown across the Atlantic and Pacific oceans by the late 1930's.

After World War II, the number of airline passengers increased sharply, both within the United States and abroad. The great change-over from propeller-driven planes to the much speedier jets in the late 1950's resulted in even more passengers. Larger, more modern airports were built to handle the growing number of passengers and planes. In the United States, airlines replaced railways as the chief means of commercial transportation.

For local travel, however, most Americans have long depended on their automobiles. This dependence eventually resulted in crowded roads and, particularly in the cities, serious air pollution. And after a fuel shortage in the mid-1970's, the cost of gasoline began to rise steadily. It soon became clear that some important changes would have to be made in cars and the ways they were used. Automobile companies were required by new laws to build cars that used less fuel and created less air pollution. The new cars were generally shorter, lighter, and had smaller engines, which meant that they would use less gasoline. And all new cars had devices that reduced the amount of pollution created by the engine. Automobile companies also began to develop cars powered by fuel-saving Diesel engines or non-polluting electric batteries.

In the cities, planners hoped to improve and expand bus service and other means of public transportation in order to decrease air pollution and relieve overcrowded expressways and streets. Some cities, such as San Francisco, built expensive new rapid-transit rail systems. Other cities studied plans to keep autos out of the main business district, thus forcing people to leave their cars at home and use public transportation.

The Story of Communication

HEARING VOICES, Big Beaver, an Indian trapper, crept silently into the bushes that fringed the hilltop. Cautiously he peered into the clearing. There, only a few yards away, sat a group of white soldiers. As soon as the soldiers were on their way, Big Beaver made a fire and began sending up a series of short smoke-puffs. His people several miles away, seeing them, immediately knew that an enemy was approaching their village.

Big Beaver's way of sending a message to his people was a common method of communication among the Indians of North America. Each tribe had its own code of signals. The smoke signals were sent from a high place, clear of trees, and from a fire built of damp grass or cedar boughs. The short puffs were made by covering and uncovering the fire with a blanket.

The early white settlers of America quickly learned what such signals meant. They, also, learned to read other messages, such as those sent at night by means of burning arrows.

Smoke and fire signals have been used by many people throughout the world. Some world events have been announced by beacon fires. Blazing fires that could be seen from hilltop to hilltop told the Greeks that King Agamemnon had taken Troy. In some parts of England memorials have been erected on the beacon hills where in 1588 fires burned to warn the people of the approach of the dreaded Spanish Armada.

The Greeks also communicated with one another by flashing their polished shields in the sunlight. The ancient Egyptians and Persians used mirrors to flash signals.

Other early forms of communication were based on man's ability to hear. One such way of spreading news was by shouting it from one man to another, each crier being stationed on a hilltop within hearing distance of the other. When Pizarro came to Peru he found wooden towers built on the mountaintops to shelter the Peruvian news criers. In colonial times it was a common practice to have a town crier shouting the time and the news on his rounds through the town.

Tapping out messages on a drum is one of the oldest methods of communication. Some African natives and South Sea Islanders still use it to relay messages from one village to the next. The first white explorers and missionaries were unable to understand how news of their coming was known long before they arrived at a native village. Later they learned that each village and tribe had its own drum station and special drummers.

From early times messages have been carried by runners. One of the greatest foot messengers was the Greek youth namd Pheidippides. He was able to run 150 miles in two days and nights.

The Romans established relay stations, with food and horses for their government riders, on the five great highways leading to Rome. Whenever the routes crossed rivers or seas, boats manned by excellent rowers were on hand to take the couriers swiftly on their way. Often the Roman armies had carrier pigeons, which could be taken by messengers into enemy country and sent back with important dispatches.

During his travels, Marco Polo found that the people of northern China had a post system whereby foot messengers, running in three-mile relays, could carry a message 100 miles in a day. Each runner wore a belt of bells in order to announce his approach in time for another runner to be ready to carry the message to the next station.

It was a great day in 1673 when the first mail carrier in colonial America set out from New York City for Boston. His route of travel was chiefly over Indian trails in the wilderness. Within a few years post riders were carrying mail from Maine to Georgia. As roads were improved, stages were used. Many of those roads over which the mail was carried are still referred to as "the old post roads."

Of all the early ways of carrying mail in the United States, none was more exciting than the Pony Express. That carrier service started at St. Louis, Missouri, and ended at Sacramento, California. Only the swiftest horses were used on the route. They were changed every ten or twenty miles. As the Pony Express messenger neared a station, the man in charge of it would have a fresh horse ready. The rider was allowed only two minutes in which to change horses. Buffalo Bill was only fifteen years old when he rode the Pony Express 380 miles in thirty-six hours.

No great improvements in the methods of communication came until Samuel F. B. Morse, a New York portrait painter, invented the telegraph, an electrical instrument by which it is possible to send messages almost instantly over wires. On May 24, 1844, the famous message "What hath God wrought" was sent from the Capitol at Washington

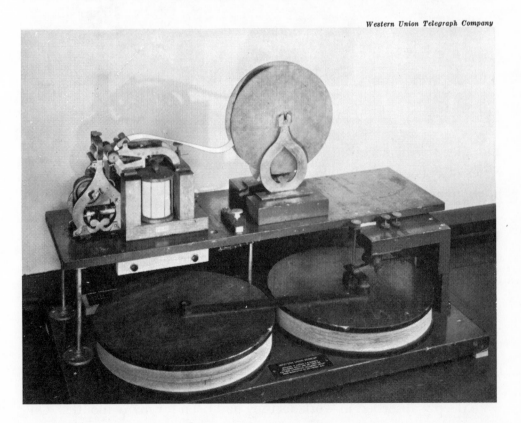

This telegraph was used by Morse to send his famous message on May 24, 1844.

American Telephone and Telegraph Company

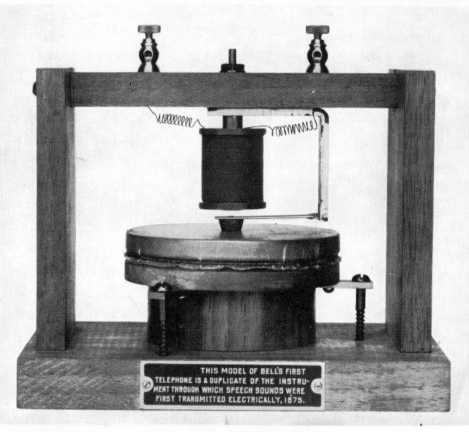

THIS MODEL OF BELL'S FIRST TELEPHONE IS A DUPLICATE OF THE INSTRUMENT THROUGH WHICH SPEECH SOUNDS WERE FIRST TRANSMITTED ELECTRICALLY, 1875.

The first telephone was invented in 1875 by Alexander Graham Bell.

and successfully received in Baltimore. That message clicked off in a series of dots and dashes, known as the Morse Code, started a new era in communication.

At first only one message at a time could be sent over a single wire. Today it is possible to send a number of messages over the same wire at the same time. In the United States alone over 2,000,000 miles of telegraph wires span the country.

By the year 1858, Cyrus W. Field had succeeded in laying a submarine telegraph line, or cable, across the Atlantic Ocean to Europe. Now many cables spanning the various oceans and seas make it possible for people to send cablegrams to distant parts of the world.

In a small Boston workshop on the tenth of March 1876, two men were deeply absorbed in work, as they had been for many months. On that particular day, one man in the attic spoke into a queer looking device, which he called a transmitter, saying, "Mr. Watson, please come here. I want you."

In a couple of minutes Mr. Watson dashed up from the basement shouting, "Mr. Bell, I heard you."

For a moment Alexander Graham Bell was speechless. At last, after years of toil and hardship, his dream of a telephone had come true.

Later that year Mr. Bell gave a public demonstration of the telephone at an exposition in Philadelphia celebrating the one hundredth anniversary of the Declaration of Independence. Even after that, it took some time to convince people that it was possible to talk into a transmitter at one end of a wire, and to be able to hear the same words through a receiver attached to the other end. Today in the United States there is about one telephone for every two people.

Greater wonders in communication were on the way. In 1895 a young Italian, Guglielmo Marconi, succeeded in sending signals by electric waves without the use of wires. His invention was none other than the wireless telegraph.

The knowledge that scientists and inventors had gathered from the inventions of the telegraph, telephone, and wireless telegraph spurred them on to discover a way to send telephone messages without wires. In time came the radio, that wonderful instrument which permits us by the snapping of a switch to fill our homes with music, or to listen to someone speaking to a world-wide audience.

The radio is a wireless telephone. Its wonder lies largely in a little glass bulb, called the audion tube, which was developed by a young wireless fan by the name of Lee De Forest. It was De Forest's invention of the audion tube that opened the way to modern radio, sound motion pictures, radar, and no doubt other miracles to come.

In the use of radar, waves are reflected back to the sender when they strike objects. Not only that, but the shape, size, and distance of the object that reflects the radar waves can be determined. For instance, radar enables airplane pilots to know whether a ship, or a mountain top, or another airplane is near, even when the object cannot be seen with the eye.

As soon as men learned to transmit speech and music through space, they began to search for a way to send pictures in somewhat the same way. The first telephotograph was sent over a wire in 1924. At the present time many newspapers use this method for securing pictures of important people and events promptly from distant parts of the country. Pictures, also, are sent by radio.

Not content to just send pictures through the air, scientists began trying to transmit moving pictures for people to enjoy in their homes. Out of their efforts came the invention of television, which name means "to see far off." Television transmits both the sound and the picture at the same moment.

We can now sit in our living rooms and actually see things that are happening in countries as far away as India. Thus television has become one of the most vital means of communication, because it has brought all the peoples of the world closer together.

Swift and efficient communication is an important part of our everyday lives. Yet in many parts of the world there are primitive people who would not believe that it is possible to talk directly to a person on the other side of the world. Modern science has produced in the field of communication instruments much more wonderful than any magic.

Television transmits both sound and picture at the same moment.

INDEX

An asterisk (*) denotes an illustration